LEAD
WITH
TRUST

A Relationship-Based Approach to Building
Happier, More Connected Workplaces

BART SPENCE

Lead With Trust:
A Relationship-Based Approach to Building Happier, More
Connected Workplaces

Published by White Fox Publishing LLC
Stockton, CA

ISBN: 979-8-9932034-0-9 (paperback)
ISBN: 979-8-9932034-1-6 (Ebook)

BUSINESS & ECONOMICS / Leadership
BUSINESS & ECONOMICS / Human Resources & Personnel Management

Cover and interior design by Asya Blue Design copyright owned by Bart Spence.

Author photograph by Kevin Richtik.

Edited by Laura Kaiser, Word Haven Editorial.
Publishing Consulting by Amanda Miller.

QUANTITY PURCHASES: Schools, companies, professional groups, clubs, and other organizations may qualify for special terms when ordering quantities of this title. For information, email info@bartspencespeaks.com

This book is lovingly dedicated

to my father-in-law, Patrick (Daddio) Shepherd. With unwavering trust, he welcomed me into his family. For his faith in me, I am forever thankful from the depths of my heart . . .

and to my brother-in-law, Joseph (Joey) Shepherd—whose devoted love for family, infectious humor, and joyful spirit inspired me throughout many pages of this book.

With love and remembrance.

CONTENTS

FOREWORD

by Tim Shepherd, CEO
Pelton Shepherd Industries

In today's fast-moving and increasingly complex business environment, trust isn't just a positive trait, it's a strategic necessity. It forms the backbone of effective leadership, strong teams, lasting customer relationships, and durable partnerships. Throughout my career, I've seen how trust accelerates collaboration, fuels innovation, and helps organizations stay steady during times of uncertainty. In industries where precision, safety, and reliability are essential, trust is what keeps teams aligned, focused, and committed to a shared mission, even when the landscape is shifting.

That's why Bart's 9 Principles of Trust resonated with me so strongly. Having worked closely with Bart, I've seen the clarity and practicality he brings to this topic. His principles aren't theoretical or abstract. They are actionable, research-driven, and shaped by deep real-world experience. Bart understands trust not just as a personal value but as a powerful leadership tool that directly affects performance, engagement, and organizational results. This book captures his expertise and his passion for building cultures where trust is practiced consistently, not just talked about.

At Pelton Shepherd Industries, many of the practices outlined in this book have already taken root, and the impact is unmistakable. Employee retention has increased by more than 40 percent, and internal surveys show a 20 percent improvement in job satisfaction. These aren't just statistics. They reflect a meaningful shift in how our teams support one another and show up for the organization. By prioritizing trust, we've become more agile, collaborative, and innovative. Engagement is higher, ideas move more freely, and people take greater ownership and pride in their work.

What sets Bart's work apart is its reach beyond the pages of this book. As a respected speaker, advisor, and thought leader, he consistently challenges leaders across industries to reconsider how trust fits into their strategic priorities. His message is clear and compelling: Trust is not a soft skill or a nice-to-have, it's a driver of real business outcomes. Whether the goal is improving operations, strengthening alignment, or deepening customer loyalty, trust is the common thread that makes sustained performance possible.

One of the greatest strengths of *Lead with Trust* is its focus on application. Bart doesn't just explain why trust matters—he shows leaders how to build it. His principles apply seamlessly in real working environments: on the manufacturing floor, where safety and quality depend on reliability; in leadership meetings, where decisions carry weight; and in organizations still shaping their culture. Each principle is grounded in lived experience and provides clear steps leaders can apply in their own contexts.

As someone who has experienced firsthand how transformative trust can be, I believe this book is not only relevant—it's essential. We are navigating an era defined by constant change, where adaptability, transparency, and strong human connection matter more than ever. *Lead with Trust* gives leaders a framework to meet these challenges with confidence and to build organizations that perform at a high level while staying true to their people.

It is with genuine respect and enthusiasm that I introduce *Lead with Trust*. Bart Spence has created a thoughtful, practical guide for leaders who are committed to leading with purpose and integrity. I hope this book serves as both a blueprint and an inspiration as you work to build stronger, more resilient organizations—where trust truly leads the way.

With trust,

Tim Shepherd

INTRODUCTION

For over twenty years, I've been living what feels like a double life, but in the best way possible. By day, I'm a human resources executive, diving headfirst into the wild, wonderful, and sometimes messy world of corporate life. It's a place where I get to roll up my sleeves, listen deeply, and bring a little clarity, compassion, and strategy to help people and organizations grow. It's more than just policies or organizational charts; it's seeing the humans behind the job titles, understanding what motivates them, and helping them discover their passion.

But when the workday winds down, I don't just kick back with a margarita and binge-watch Netflix (although, trust me, that's tempting). Instead, I dive into my other passion, the one that makes my heart race and my soul light up: public speaking and leadership coaching. This is where I get to trade the boardroom for a stage and pour everything I've got into helping people become leaders who not only lead but also inspire. I'm not here to churn out cookie-cutter bosses who chase titles or corner offices. No, my mission is to help people lead with authenticity, purpose, and a great deal of joy.

I've been in the leadership game for over two decades, and I've seen it all: the triumphs, the missteps, the breakthroughs, and the "Oh crap, let's never do *that* again" setbacks. Through countless coffee-fueled conversations, late-night strategy sessions, and those inspiring moments when a leader finally *gets it*, I've learned one undeniable truth: Success, no matter how alluring it looks on paper, feels hollow without joy. It's like winning a shiny trophy that looks epic under the spotlight but feels cold and weightless in your hands: no warmth, no soul, no *life*.

So, what's the secret ingredient that breathes life into success? Relationships. Not the shallow, "let's grab a quick coffee and exchange business cards" kind. I'm referring to the real deal: those brave, beautiful, and sometimes gloriously imperfect connections built on trust. These are the bonds that not only survive the challenges of life and work but also thrive in it. They're the ones that make you laugh until your sides hurt, lift you up when you're down, and remind you why you keep showing up, day after day.

Let me take you back to a simpler time. Imagine grass-stained jeans, sunburned noses, and the pure, unfiltered joy of a playground at recess. I was seven years old, and my best friend and I were absolute *legends* on the teeter-totter. You know the one—that creaky, wooden contraption that was equal parts thrill ride and physics lesson until some lawyers deemed it a liability. When we got it right, it was spectacular: one of us soaring to the sky, the other dipping low, then switching places in perfect rhythm. We'd push off the ground with just the right force, reading each other's moves like we shared a secret telepathic language. For those glorious moments, we were invincible.

But the thing about teeter-totters is that they're unforgiving teachers. If one of us got distracted, say, by a rogue ice cream truck, or if our timing was off, or worst of all, if someone bailed mid-ride? Well, prepare for impact, complete with a bruised bottom, and that sinking, "what just happened?" feeling. This is a relationship, a relationship that requires a balance of give and take. And the unsung hero of the whole operation? The fulcrum. That humble little pivot point didn't beg for attention, but without it our teeter-totter was just a sad plank of wood, destined for the firewood pile.

In the grand and sometimes chaotic dance of relationships, trust is that fulcrum. It's the quiet, steady force that keeps everything from collapsing into a shambles. No trust? No balance. No balance? No joy. Before long, you're sitting in your corner office or eyeing that impressive paycheck, asking yourself, *Is this really all there is?*

RELATIONSHIPS

TRUST

The Journey to Trust

My obsession with trust didn't come from a textbook or a motivational poster. It's been an exciting and winding journey, forged in the heat of real-world mayhem, boardroom showdowns, team meltdowns, make-or-break turnarounds, and everything in between. Throughout my career as an HR professional and leadership coach, I've collaborated with hundreds of leaders, from scrappy startup founders to Fortune 500 executives, both individually and in group settings, to uncover avenues for skill-building and self-reflection. And I've seen what happens when trust is rock-solid and what happens when it's shaky. Through it all, I've distilled what I've learned into something I'm incredibly excited to share: The 9 Principles of Trust.

These aren't vague theories or buzzword bingo. They're battle-tested, practical truths, shaped by years of experience and proven by extraordinary leaders who've used them to rally loyal teams, crush ambitious goals, and stay true to their values, even when the pressure is on. The 9 Principles are my roadmap for building rock-solid relationships. They're centered on forging a rhythm of trust that empowers you to navigate life and work with confidence, grace, and joy.

The 9 Principles Are Born

About fifteen years ago, I was the HR director at a fast-growing manufacturing company. Part of my routine was checking in with new hires to see how they were settling in, what was going well, and where they might be facing challenges. That's how I met Emily, a sharp, driven leader we'd recently brought on to head our research and development team. She was full of innovative ideas, and her arrival had generated a great deal of excitement about the changes she might bring.

But during our one-on-one, it quickly became clear that her experience didn't quite match the optimism. "So, Emily, it's nice to finally meet you. How have things been going?" I asked, leaning back in my chair, expecting the usual new-hire enthusiasm. Instead, she gave a lukewarm, "Eh, it's okay, I guess." Oof. I could sense the hesitation immediately. A heaviness crept in—quiet but unmistakable, the kind that makes you brace for what might come next.

I decided to dig a little deeper. "What's up? Is something wrong? Want to talk about it?" After a long pause, she finally opened up. She was struggling to trust her manager. Let's call him Andy.

"Trust him to do what?" I leaned in, pressing, my curiosity piqued. Her blank stare clearly revealed her reservations about speaking up. So, I threw out a curveball to shake things up and lighten the mood a bit. "Well, would you trust Andy to park your car?" She grinned, a hint of energy breaking through. "I'm not sure anyone would want to be seen in that old clunker." "Okay, what about babysitting your kids?" I asked. "No way!" she laughed, her guard dropping. "It would take a long time to earn that kind of trust—my standards for that gig are off the chart."

That conversation revealed a deep, fundamental truth: Trust isn't a starting point or some inherent value you slap on like a bumper sticker. It's a *result*, something you build, little by little, through consistent, legitimate experiences. It's not enough to say, "Trust me!" and expect people to fall in line. Trust is earned through actions, not words, and it's as fragile as it is powerful.

I pushed further, asking Emily to share her experience with Andy. What she revealed was disappointing, to put it mildly. During her hiring process, Andy had promised that she could take a planned vacation four months into her role, a family trip she had been looking forward to for years. It was a dealbreaker for her, and Andy's assurance sealed her decision to join the team. However, when she submitted her PTO request months later, Andy shut it down cold, citing "not enough accrued time"—the classic bait and switch. Worse, he began dodging her one-on-one meetings, offering vague excuses, and sidelining her in team meetings, leaving her ideas ignored and her confidence in his leadership crumbling.

That story lit a fire within me. Not only had Andy broken a promise, he'd also compounded the harm by shutting Emily out, eroding the very foundation of their working relationship. It was a textbook case of trust gone AWOL. So, I rolled up my sleeves and began coaching Andy. For weeks, we focused on fulfilling commitments, being transparent, leading by example, and demonstrating personal accountability, among other key priorities for building trust.

It wasn't long after that when the 9 Principles of Trust emerged, a powerful framework designed to empower leaders in forging trust-based relationships and cultivating cultures of fulfillment.

Emily sent a postcard from Cabo: "My family says thank you, we're having a great time. Expect a bottle of tequila soon!" The empty bottle still sits in my office, serving as a subtle reminder of the power and importance of building trust.

Beyond the Principles

The 9 Principles of trust aren't just another corporate tool—they're a roadmap for building deeper, more meaningful connections in all areas of life. I've seen these principles transform relationships beyond the workplace, rejuvenating marriages, prompting joy in friendships, and even helping parents and children understand each other better.

Trust is the core element that makes every relationship thrive with possibility. And the best part? You don't need any special qualifications to start. Whether you're leading a team, forming a new friendship, or just striving to become a better version of yourself, these principles offer a solid foundation. Plus, it's never too late to dive in; trust is always ready to meet you where you are.

Batter Up

It was 2012, a pivotal moment that changed one man's path, as both a leader and a father. As the HR director at our company,

I was guiding Javier, a promising young executive, through his turbulent early days of leadership. Recent setbacks had eroded his team's faith in him, leaving him isolated and doubting his own potential. Together, we explored the fundamentals of trust-building: fostering transparent conversations, honoring every commitment, celebrating successes with genuine praise, and unlocking the unexpected power of shared laughter. Slowly but surely, he transformed. His confidence blossomed, his team reciprocated with loyalty, and mutual respect began to permeate their work.

Yet the true trigger of inspiration extended beyond the office walls. One afternoon, Javier came into my office. His voice was steady, but his eyes brimmed with emotion. What he shared wasn't about spreadsheets or strategies—it was a heartfelt testament to how these lessons had mended the most precious bond in his life: his relationship with his young son.

As an up-and-comer in the corporate world, he'd been consumed with endless meetings and deadlines, missing game after game of his son's Little League baseball season. Each absence chipped away at their connection, until his son began to doubt Dad's word on anything at all. The weight of that lost trust hung heavy, a silent fracture in their family.

However, here's where the story takes a turn. Armed with the simple yet profound principle of keeping commitments, he refused to let work define him. He reshuffled his calendar, carved out time, delegated various time-consuming tasks to his team, and showed up for the final three games of the season. Weeks later, as the season's dust settled, Javier's son hugged him and thanked him for coming to the games. Javier knew that trust had been reignited.

As Javier recounted the story, he fought back his emotions. In that moment, I didn't see a leader who'd conquered a boardroom, I saw a father who'd reclaimed the trust in his son's eyes.

It reminded me that true leadership begins at home, with the courage to show up, follow through, and let vulnerability be your greatest strength. No matter how overwhelming life's demands may be, one committed step can heal wounds, restore faith, and inspire a legacy of trust.

Javier's story isn't just a touching reminder of the power of personal commitment—it's also a mirror for what great leadership looks like today. In many ways, his choice to show up for his son reflects the exact shift the professional world has had to make in recent years: from managing tasks to showing genuine care, from control to trust, and from rigid systems to human-centered leadership. That shift became especially clear during one of the most disruptive events in modern history—COVID-19.

A Change in Landscape

Since the pandemic hit, the way we work has changed in a significant and lasting way. Companies had to quickly rethink how they operated, while employees began to see work—and the workplace—very differently. The rapid shift to remote and hybrid work forced organizations to let go of the old mindset that work only happens in an office under direct supervision. Instead, we saw a move toward more flexible, trust-based ways of working, where autonomy and accountability matter more than simply being physically present.

With managers no longer able to keep an eye on everyone in person, the focus naturally shifted from clocking in hours to actually getting things done. That meant trusting people to manage their own time, stay productive, and hit their goals—often without anyone looking over their shoulder. For many, this exposed just how outdated some traditional work models were, and it made a strong case for giving people more control over how they work.

At the same time, employees around the world started asking bigger questions about what they really wanted from their jobs. The Great Resignation wasn't just about quitting—it was about leaving behind toxic cultures, rigid schedules, and constant burn-out. More than ever, people began to prioritize mental health, work-life balance, and a sense of purpose. It stopped being just about the paycheck. People wanted to work for companies that respected their time, energy, and values.

These two major shifts—how companies run, and what employees expect—have pushed businesses to change. To stay competitive and attract great talent, organizations are realizing they need to create cultures built on trust, empathy, and open communication. Today's leaders need more than just technical know-how—they need to build environments where people feel safe, supported, and free to be themselves.

Trust isn't just a nice-to-have anymore—it's essential. It keeps remote teams connected, drives engagement, and encourages innovation and collaboration. It plays a huge role in team per-formance, employee loyalty, and even a company's reputation.

The bottom line is, workers now expect more. More flexibility, more humanity, and a lot more trust. The companies that get this—and build trust into everything they do—aren't just adapt-ing. They're setting themselves up to thrive in the future of work.

So, here's my challenge: Take a moment to pause. Take a deep, no-filter look at the relationships in your life. Focus on the bonds that connect you to your coworkers, family, ride-or-die crew, or even to yourself. Where is trust standing tall, shining like a lighthouse? Where is it shaky, perhaps in need of a little TLC?

Now, choose a relationship that inspires you or touches your heart, and focus on just one of the 9 Principles. Perhaps it's keeping your word and showing up on time without making flimsy excuses. Or maybe it's radical honesty, removing the mask and sharing your quirks, dreams, or that one fear you pretend doesn't exist. Or possibly empowering others, taking the chance to trust someone to lead and supporting them without hovering like a helicopter parent. Whatever principle you choose to start with, dive in with everything you have. Commit to it with intention, a dose of bravery, and a determination to reach beyond mediocrity.

Don't stress over crafting an epic, dramatic move. Trust grows in the small, everyday moments that accumulate over time. You show up day after day, stacking those tiny bricks of trust until you've built a fortress that can withstand any attack.

As you lean into this, keep your eyes peeled for opportunity. Observe how the landscape shifts, perhaps your friend opens up more, or your team operates in sync. Recognize how the connection feels warmer, steadier.

When trust becomes the foundation, the relationship takes flight. It transforms into a source of laughter, strength, and joy. The journey may have its bumps, missed steps, and awkward moments, but it's a wild, fantastic ride, proof that something as simple as trust can change how we connect. So, grab your principle and leap into the adventure. Trust is waiting to illuminate your life, one joyful, deliberate step at a time.

CHAPTER ONE: THE 1ST PRINCIPLE

OPEN AND HONEST COMMUNICATION

Picture a workplace where ideas flow freely, every voice is heard, and honesty is not the exception. That's the power of open and honest communication—it's not just desirable, it's a foundational element of a healthy and effective team. When people feel safe to speak up, offer feedback, or respectfully challenge ideas, collaboration improves, innovation thrives, and trust grows stronger. Over time, what might have started as just a typical office becomes something more: a workplace where people are genuinely engaged, aligned, and motivated to succeed together.

The Tie That Changed Everything

Years ago, a manufacturing giant in Northern California hired me as a consultant to revitalize their leadership. The diagnosis was clear: They needed raw honesty, fearless openness, and a touch of humor. During a weeklong workshop, we broke down barriers, forged strong connections, and redefined how leadership interacted with one another and with their teams. The results were transformative—trust surged, morale escalated, and the company's culture began to stir with potential.

But the real fireworks erupted a few months later when the CEO, Brad, reached out to me. Brad had skipped the workshop, but he had seen the effects: a leadership team now radiating positivity and achieving their goals. The issue was that Brad had a personal challenge. With a make-or-break quarterly company review looming, he confessed that his focused, stone-cold, "don't talk to me" demeanor was creating distance with employees instead of firing them up. This, coupled with the reality of presenting some bad news to board members, had him feeling a bit apprehensive. He needed some help, and he needed it fast.

With just two days to create some brilliance, I coached Brad in the art of genuine human connection. We devised a high-energy game plan: Embrace your quirks, share a personal story, and communicate with guts and emotion. I left with my fingers crossed, hoping for the best, until I was invited to watch Brad's quarterly review.

Brad took the stage like a man on a mission, his polished shoes clicking against the hardwood with a rhythm that radiated confidence. He didn't just walk, he strutted—shoulders back, chin held high, exuding a swagger that could charm a room or make it bristle. The auditorium was a pressure cooker, rows of employees sat stiffly in their chairs, eyes darting to the floor or glued to their laptops, faces marked by the kind of nervous anticipation that arises when you know the numbers aren't good. The fluorescent lights burned dimly overhead, casting a sterile glow over the sea of navy blazers and muted ties.

Brad positioned himself front and center, gripping the edges of the lectern for a brief moment before stepping out from behind it. No barriers. Just him, the mic clipped to his lapel, and a crowd waiting for the axe to fall. He scanned the room slowly and deliberately, his sharp blue eyes catching glints of worry, judgment, boredom, and the occasional smirk. Then, he dropped his opener: "Look, we all know this quarter's been a dumpster fire."

The room froze. A few people shifted in their seats, one guy in the back coughed nervously, and a woman in the third row stopped mid-sip of her coffee, her cup hovering awkwardly. Brad let the silence linger for a moment, just long enough to make everyone squirm, before he leaned forward, his voice dropping as if he were letting them in on a secret. "But before we dive into the grim details of spreadsheets and sales targets, let's talk about the real elephant in the room."

Every head shot up. Eyes widened, brows arched, and curiosity ran through the crowd. Was he going to call out the layoffs nobody wanted to mention? The botched inventory that was still the talk of the breakroom? Nobody knew, and that uncertainty hooked them like fish on a line.

Brad paused, savoring the moment, his lips curling into a sly grin. Then, with the timing of a seasoned comic, he delivered the punchline: "My ties."

A collective blink. A few confused glances were exchanged. Did he say "ties"?

"Yeah, you heard me," he said, his voice steady but his eyes twinkling with mischief, like a kid who'd just pulled off the perfect prank. "I know they're loud, tacky, and a total fashion crime—I'm not blind. I also know I'm the butt of your jokes, your water cooler whispers, and probably a meme or two floating around the office." He stepped forward, flicking the tie dangling from his neck, a chaotic burst of crimson, violet, and neon yellow, woven into a design that screamed pure anarchy. "I mean, come on, this one looks like I was attacked and tagged by a bat-crazy graffiti artist."

The room erupted with laughter. Chairs squeaked as people leaned forward, clutching their sides. The guy in the back who'd coughed earlier was now red-faced, slapping his knee. Even the stoic VP in the front row, who hadn't cracked a smile since the Clinton administration, let out a low chuckle. The tension that had gripped the room moments ago exploded like confetti, scattering in every direction.

Brad stood there, soaking it in, his grin widening as he watched the crowd unravel. He raised a hand, signaling for quiet, but the laughter lingered. When the room settled, he softened, his voice dropping to a warmer, more intimate tone, as if he were talking with a friend over coffee. "But here's the thing," he said, his eyes sweeping the room, connecting with as many faces as possible. "My wife picks these ties. Every single one. She loves them. Thinks they're gutsy, fun, a statement. And you know what? I love my wife. So, I wear them. Even if they make me look like I got dressed in a clown's laundry basket."

A few soft laughs drifted through the crowd, and the mood had shifted.

People were leaning in now, not just entertained but intrigued. Brad paced slowly across the stage, his hands in his pockets, the tie swinging slightly with each step. "Sometimes," he continued, "you take one for the team. Even if it bruises your pride, you push through, because this isn't centered on you. It's for a greater purpose."

He stopped, turning to face the crowd head-on, his voice steady but laced with conviction. "That's what I would like our focus to be today. Not just numbers or quotas or the fact that our competitors are breathing down our necks. I'm here to discuss how we, as a company, can make courageous, selfless moves for one another and our customers. How we can take the hit, wear the ugly tie, and show up anyway, because that's what builds trust. That's what builds loyalty. That's what turns a rough quarter into a comeback story."

The room was silent now, but it wasn't the heavy, anxious silence from before—it was the kind of silence that resonates with attention, with possibility. Brad let it linger, his eyes scanning the crowd one last time before he stepped back to the lectern, ready to dive into the numbers, but not before he'd made damn sure everyone in that room was with him, ugly tie and all. By the end, employees he had never met approached him with ideas, questions, and admiration for his candor. It wasn't just a meeting—it was a cultural revolution.

Developing the first principle involves multiple elements, including open and honest communication, moral courage, practicing active listening, and more. Let's get going!

A Case Study in Guts and Charm

Brad's story demonstrates how a leader's openness, via unfiltered candor, self-deprecating humor, and heartfelt honesty, can dismantle obstacles, restore confidence, and create shared energy, even in the face of tough updates. At its heart, the takeaway is that genuine dialogue goes beyond mere information—it involves revealing your own humanity to infuse the situation with empathy, transforming possible alienation into rapport.

Let's examine each element that contributed to the effectiveness of Brad's approach in greater depth.

Open and Honest Communication

Brad kicked off by saying, "We all know this quarter's been a dumpster fire," calling out the setback head-on rather than sugarcoating it.

Lesson learned: This echoes the principle of open and honest communication, which breathed new life into the leadership team. Being candid begins with acknowledging everyday hardships, which eases tension before it builds up. It avoids the icy "don't approach me" demeanor that breeds isolation, instead of signaling to your team that you're right there in the fight alongside them.

The result: The audience's early stiffness melted into active involvement, demonstrating how candidness grabs focus and builds commitment, as evidenced by the sharp rise in trust and spirits after the session.

Using Humor to Lower Defenses

Brad pivoted to his tacky ties, admitting they're a fashion crime. Laughter erupted, transforming tension into release.

Lesson learned: Humor, especially at your own expense, disarms skepticism and signals approachability. This approach demonstrates that vulnerability fosters safety rather than weakness.

The result: Even the stoic VP chuckled, and the crowd leaned in, evidence that levity converts passive listeners into active participants.

Sharing Personal Vulnerability to Build Empathy

Brad revealed that his wife picks the ties and he wears them because he loves her, framing it as a selfless move despite the embarrassment. He tied this to the company's need for courageous, team-first actions.

Lesson learned: Openness about quirks or flaws invited an exchange, shifting focus from individual ego to collective purpose. It embodied genuine human connection and guts and emotion, countering Brad's pre-coaching apprehension.

The result: The mood evolved from anxious silence to one of echoing attention, with employees approaching him afterward, proving that vulnerability creates loyalty and fosters ideas.

Connecting the Personal to the Professional

Brad linked the tie metaphor to business challenges: "Take the hit, wear the ugly tie, and show up anyway," to build trust and turn setbacks into comeback stories.

Lesson learned: Honest communication thrives when it weaves personal anecdotes into actionable insights, inspiring others to mirror that courage.

The result: The presentation ended not with dread but with possibility, leading to unsolicited engagement, a direct outcome of framing honesty as a tool for moral courage and loyalty.

Overall Impact and Tie to Leadership Principles

The story demonstrates open communication as a multiplier, escalating morale and transforming a pressure cooker into a launchpad. By blending honesty, humor, and heart, Brad embodied the first principle's elements, active listening (via eye contact and pauses), moral courage (admitting flaws publicly), and more, proving that leaders who show up anyway don't just deliver news—they deliver transformation. This wasn't soft idealism—it was substantiated by a ripple effect, from isolated CEO to admired influencer, triggering a cultural revolution in under an hour.

1. Moral Courage

I am a classic last-minute shopper. It was 2023, two days before Christmas, and I was at a women's clothing store. I cannot say where, that would be impolite . . . let's just call it Needless Markups. The place was chaotic. While waiting in line, I noticed a woman causing a scene at the checkout over what appeared to be a pricing debacle. She was berating the cashier with personal insults, reducing her to tears, and demanding to see the manager. When the manager arrived, I caught snippets of the woman's tirade, including the infamous line, "I'm the customer, and the customer is always right." The manager, visibly torn, looked at the cashier and other staff. She stayed silent until the woman snapped, "Well? Are you going to fix this?" The manager replied, "Yes, I am." After a pause, she added, "I'm asking you to leave, but first, please apologize to Sarah." I was floored, such moral courage! The woman didn't apologize, but it didn't matter. The manager took the more challenging path, stood up for her team, and did what was right.

When I arrived at the counter, the manager was still there. "That was a tough call, huh?" I said. Hesitating, she replied, "Well, it was. I'm sure I'll catch hell for it when my district manager hears about it." I paused, looked her in the eye, and said, "What you did back there was remarkable. You stood up for your team and showed real courage, even knowing it might come at a cost. That kind of action inspires people." Her eyes welled up, and I could tell she felt the weight of what she had done. I was just grateful to have witnessed it.

Embracing humor to lighten the situation, I jokingly questioned the absurd price of the items I was purchasing. Her tears turned into laughter.

Moral courage doesn't mean you are free from fear or doubt. As Nelson Mandela eloquently stated in his autobiography, *Long Walk to Freedom*, "I learned that courage was not the absence of fear, but the triumph over it." As a leader, you stand at a crossroads. You can either embrace the discomfort of transparency, tackling the inevitable conflicts head-on, or opt for the easier path of concealment, hoping to maintain a fleeting sense of calm.

As the retail manager demonstrated, true moral courage lies in choosing the more challenging path, upholding your principles with unwavering integrity, even when the risks are high. By consistently aligning your actions with your values, you forge a reputation rooted in authenticity and resilience, earning the respect and trust of those you lead.

This kind of skilled leadership isn't a one-time effort—it's more like a muscle that grows stronger each time you face tough decisions and real-world challenges. Every time you choose the difficult but honorable path, you build resilience and expand your impact. From personal experience, I can tell you that it's not always comfortable—but it is gratifying. There's a unique sense of pride and fulfillment that comes from standing firm in your values when it matters most.

The Path to Moral Courage

To begin your path to building moral courage, I recommend starting by identifying what truly matters to you, your core values.

These are the guiding principles that shape your decisions, your sense of right and wrong, and ultimately, your actions in difficult situations. When you're clear about your values, you're more likely to act with integrity, even when it's uncomfortable or risky. Here are some steps to help you with this exercise.

Discovering Your Core Values

Knowing your core values starts with being real with yourself. It means slowing down and taking a good honest look—not just at who you are but at what actually matters to you deep down. It's not just about picking traits you think sound good—it's about discovering the beliefs that drive your choices, shape your relationships, and define who you are.

Start by carving out some quiet time without distractions. Think back on moments when you felt especially proud, fulfilled, or even really frustrated. Those intense emotions can be great clues to what you genuinely care about.

To get going, jot down five to ten words or short phrases that really resonate with you. Think about things like honesty, fairness, compassion, loyalty, freedom, growth, creativity—whatever feels true to you. Don't overthink it—go with your gut. But if you get stuck, try asking yourself:

- What really ticks me off? Why?
- Who do I admire most? What do they stand for?
- What kind of mark do I want to leave on the world?
- What would I stand up for, even if it cost me something?

As you reflect, you'll probably notice some themes popping up—maybe a strong pull toward fairness, connection, or staying true to yourself. Those patterns can help you name your values more clearly.

Keep in mind that your values aren't just goals or ideals—they're the core beliefs you already try to live by, even if you're still figuring them out. Once you're clear on them, you can start making choices that actually line up with what matters to you.

Write Your Own Personal Values Statement

Try turning your values into a short, clear statement—something like: "I stand for justice by speaking up for those who aren't heard, even when it's uncomfortable." Keep it somewhere you'll see it often, such as your phone's lock screen or your desk. It's a great way to stay grounded in what matters most—especially when things get messy.

I have done this exercise, and I can tell you it was enlightening and empowering. Taking the time to reflect on what I truly believe in has helped me make clearer, more informed decisions, especially when faced with moral or ethical challenges. To assist you on your own journey of self-discovery, I'll share my personal value statement. I hope that it offers inspiration or a starting point as you begin to define your own.

In no particular order, here are the core values that guide me:

- **Family:** I commit to maintaining a work-life balance, even when the pressures of work escalate.

- **Empathy:** I commit to treating others with genuine care and understanding, free from judgment.

- **Leadership by example:** I commit to exhibiting exactly the behavior I expect from others.

- **Positivity:** I commit to maintaining a positive attitude and outlook even during challenging times.

- **Impact:** I commit to helping the world become a happier place to work.

Here are a couple of additional steps you can take to help incorporate moral courage into your everyday leadership and personal life.

Reflecting on past decisions: Think back on three to five key moments in your life or career where a decision you made—or didn't make—stuck with you. These could be times you're proud of, moments you regret, or choices that still weigh on your mind. For each, take a few minutes to reflect on these questions.

- **What happened?** Recall the situation clearly— what was going on, how you felt, who was involved, and what the main decision point was. Was it personal, professional, or ethical?

- **What values were involved?** Which of your core values came into play? Did your actions line up with what matters most to you—like honesty, compassion, or fairness? Or did you feel tension between what you did and what you believe in?

- **What was the result?** Look at the short- and long-term impact of your choice. How did it affect you and others? Did it change the way you see yourself or influence your relationships or work?

- **What would you change?** If the moment still brings regret or unease, think about how you'd handle it differently now. What actions would better reflect your values? Try to reframe the moment with a more aligned response.

Example: Let's say during a meeting, someone made a biased joke and you stayed silent—even though inclusion matters to you. Think about what held you back (fear of conflict or not knowing what to say), and how you could respond next time. Maybe with a calm, redirecting comment like: "Hey, let's keep it inclusive—I've got a better one." This gives you a go-to response that reflects your values without escalating tension.

When Moral Courage is Challenged

As a leader, there may come a time when your values, beliefs, or moral courage are tested—especially by those in upper leadership. Whether it's a decision that doesn't sit right with you, a directive that feels misaligned with your principles, or pressure to compromise on something important, these moments can be some of the most challenging you'll face. They're not just professional dilemmas—they're personal tests of character. How you respond can shape your leadership legacy, your credibility, and even your future career path.

Here are some practical tips to help you navigate these difficult situations with both integrity and effectiveness.

Know what you stand for: Before you're ever put in a tough spot, be clear on your values. When you know where you stand, you're more likely to respond with confidence—not just emotion. Take time to reflect on what lines you're not willing to cross, both personally and professionally.

Seek first to understand: Not every challenged value is what it seems. Sometimes it's just a misunderstanding or a breakdown in communication. Ask questions to get the complete picture before reacting, such as, "Can you help me understand what you meant when you said that?" This shows maturity and might even reveal common ground.

Take a pause: Don't let frustration take the wheel. Give yourself space to process and think it through. Use statements to explain where you're coming from, something like: "I'm a little concerned this could go against our commitment to transparency. Can we talk through some other options?"

Bring solutions: If you're going to challenge a decision, come prepared with ideas that move things forward. Demonstrate how your suggestion aligns with both your personal values and the organization's broader objectives—such as trust, long-term success, or reputation.

Reach out to your support system: You don't have to figure it all out alone. Consult with a mentor, a trusted colleague, or a representative in HR. Sometimes just having a sounding board can help you see things more clearly and make more intelligent choices.

You might one day face a choice between following orders and standing by what you believe is right. Standing by your values could come with consequences—but in the long run, it's about the kind of leader (and person) you want to be. Even if others fall short, you can still lead with integrity. Your team is watching. How you handle these moments speaks volumes about your character and leadership.

2. Leading by Example

Leading by example is a timeless strategy that continues to be valued by business owners, executives, and managers as a crucial skill for effective communication, building trust, and achieving team success. It involves embodying the values, work ethic, and behaviors you want your team to reflect, such as honesty, responsibility, and authenticity.

I once worked with an executive who loved to rally the team with big speeches that pertained to our company's core values: integrity, teamwork, honesty, the works. He'd stand at the front of the room, all charisma, preaching how we should live these principles every day. But then you'd see him in action: cutting corners, playing favorites, or dodging accountability when things got tough. It was like watching a bad actor in a play he didn't believe in. Every time he pulled that stunt, I'd mentally paraphrase a famous idea from Ralph Waldo Emerson: "Your actions speak so loudly, I can't hear what you're saying." It was the perfect reminder that words don't mean much when your behavior tells a different story.

It has been well documented that Walt Disney, the visionary behind both groundbreaking animation and the modern theme park, was a perfectionist who lived out his values through his actions. In the early days of Disneyland, during the 1950s and 1960s, Walt was often seen pausing his stroll through the park to pick up litter—a gum wrapper here, a cigarette butt there. He never made a show of it, but his quiet example spoke volumes. If you ever visit Disneyland, as I have many times, you'll notice one thing: It's spotless. That's the power of leading by example.

Lead through your actions. Don't just speak about high standards, live them. When you show up with integrity, consistency, and authenticity, your team will take note. When they see you holding yourself accountable, staying true to your values, and doing the hard work, they'll be more inclined to do the same, not out of obligation but because they're inspired to. Your actions set the tone, creating a culture built on trust, initiative, and mutual respect. Walk the talk; the chain reaction starts with you.

Here are some steps you can take to help you on your path to embracing this valuable principle.

Owning It

In a world fixated on picture-perfect leaders, it's tempting to hide mistakes, dodge blame, or stall progress. However, authentic leadership has nothing to do with a flawless image (thanks, social media). It's embracing our chaotic humanity! Trust comes from authenticity, not a polished facade.

To illustrate this point, I've considered starting a Facebook page dedicated to sharing my biggest blunders, crummy meals, awkward photos, and the dull places I've visited. Maybe instead of Facebook, I'll create a new site called Faceplant. Yeah, you're right, that's probably a bit grim, but at least it'd be authentic!

When you stumble, and you will, don't brush it off with a casual "My bad" and move on. Own it. Roll up your sleeves, step into the mess with your team, and face what went wrong head-on. Show them what accountability really looks like. Be the one who leads the charge toward a more innovative, stronger way forward. Missed an output target? Skip the vague "We fell short." Instead, identify the root cause, whether it's outdated equipment holding you back, understaffing due to delayed hiring, or a supply chain bottleneck.

That kind of honesty takes guts, but it also builds trust. When your team sees you confront failure with courage and transparency, they'll feel safe to do the same. No need to aim for perfection, just show up genuine, grounded, and with purpose.

Let me share a moment that still sticks with me.

I worked with an incredible plant manager named Kevin, a leader I genuinely admired for his grit and authenticity. One month, things didn't go as planned, and Kevin found himself facing a significant shortfall in his monthly production quota. That's the kind of situation that can make even the most seasoned leader sweat, but Kevin addressed it with courage and clarity.

I vividly remember him pulling me aside, his brow furrowed but his resolve unshaken. "I've got a tough conversation coming up with the team," he said, his voice steady but searching. "Any advice on how to handle it?" Already aware of his situation, I looked him in the eye and kept it simple: "Kevin, just be yourself, keep it real, and own it. That's all they need from you." He nodded, took a deep breath, and stepped into the meeting room with confidence.

"All right, everyone," he began, his tone calm yet commanding attention. "I messed this one up. I miscalculated, plain and simple. I underestimated the maintenance demands of our aging conveyor system and failed to hire enough skilled technicians in time to keep things running smoothly. That led to downtime, and we fell short of our goal. But I have a plan. We're addressing this head-on, and I need your input to make it right."

Boom, that was it! No excuses, no sugarcoating, and not over-complicated. That moment wasn't just about accepting responsibility and owning the mistake—it also helped build trust and rally the team. Kevin's candid approach built credibility and helped to encourage a team of problem-solvers. The group didn't just hear him—they felt his commitment. They rolled up their sleeves, collaborated on solutions, and tackled challenges with renewed purpose.

When production targets, or any critical goals for that matter, take a hit, don't dodge or deflect. Step up, communicate the issue with clear precision, pinpoint the specific causes, and lay out a plan for corrective action. Kevin showed me that day what it means to lead with heart and hustle, and it's a lesson I carry with me every day. Because when you own it, you inspire others to rise and own it too, driving progress that not only meets but exceeds expectations.

Map Out a Solution with Precision

Owning your stumble takes bravery and is seriously commendable. However, when you pivot into action, that's when the real magic happens. It's time to chart the path forward and lay out your next steps with clarity and confidence. Reallocate resources, tweak timelines, or introduce new processes that not only solve the issue but make your team say, "Now that's how it's done." This is your chance to turn a setback into momentum, so make the most of it. Here's how.

Chart the course for swift recovery: Start by dissecting the chaos into small, actionable next steps that align everyone. Ask the tough questions: What's the immediate pivot to steady the ship? Perhaps it's a resource reallocation to address those glaring gaps, drawing talent from lower-priority areas to where it's needed most. Or maybe a timeline tweak that preserves momentum without burning out the team, trimming fat without slashing muscle.

Spell it out in no uncertain terms, making it concrete and trackable: "By EOD Friday, we'll reallocate Team Bravo's bandwidth to high-impact tasks like client outreach and prototype testing, shaving two weeks off our recovery curve and locking in that Q4 milestone." Document it in a strategy room so no one's left guessing.

Elevate fixes into epic upgrades: Sure, fixing the leak stops the flood, but why settle for basic when you've got the chance to transform the entire system? This is your moment to go beyond the bandage and turn recovery into reinvention. Don't just restore order, elevate it. Inject your fix with that signature flair that sets your leadership style apart.

Think bigger. Introduce a solution that not only addresses the immediate issue but also levels up how your team operates moving forward. Maybe it's launching a collaborative dashboard that tracks real-time wins, visualizes progress, and keeps everyone aligned and motivated. Picture your team logging in and seeing their efforts move the needle, progress bars climbing, tasks clearing, and small victories stacking up. That's not just solving a problem—that's creating momentum.

These kinds of upgrades evoke innovation, boost morale, and turn your team into cocreators of a brighter, more dynamic future. Now that's leadership on a whole new level!

Fuel the journey: No journey toward excellence is a solo mission. To truly move forward you need an inspired crew at your side. So, rally your team with energy that not only grabs attention but also earns their trust and engagement. Set the tone right from the start. Kick things off with a focused, energizing team huddle—fifteen minutes max, whether virtual or in person. Use this moment to share your vision and reveal your game plan with clarity and confidence. Highlight early wins to build momentum. Say something like "Shout-out to the development team, we nailed the beta launch two days early!" That kind of public recognition goes further than you think. Make it personal. Make it real.

But don't stop there, back it up with small, consistent moments of appreciation. A surprise coffee run or a personal acknowledgment can go a long way. These mini celebrations help build team spirit and maintain high motivation, especially during high-pressure phases.

As the plan unfolds, keep your ears open. Actively listen to feedback and remain open to making adjustments. Flexibility demonstrates that you're not just leading but also cocreating the path forward. And always bring it back to the bigger picture: how this shift, challenge, or pivot is making the team stronger, more adaptable, and better equipped for the future.

The Power of Self-Reflection

Leading by example means living up to the standards you require of others. The saying "Take a look in the mirror" captures what self-awareness in leadership is about: regularly examining your own actions, choices, and their impact on your team or organization.

If you skip this honest self-check, you can end up ignoring your weaknesses. This often leads to unmotivated teams, weak results, or even the whole organization falling apart. Authentic leadership requires being open and brave enough to face harsh realities about yourself.

I'll break this down further with simple questions to help you assess yourself, along with clear signs to gauge the effectiveness of your leadership. Together, these tools provide a solid plan to make tangible improvements.

- Am I leading by example? Are you showing up the way you expect others to? Think about how often you're on time, how openly you communicate, and how you handle pressure. For example, if you say you value work-life balance but you're sending late-night emails, what message are you actually sending? Take a look at your day-to-day habits— are they reinforcing the standards you expect from your team, or quietly undercutting them?

- How does my presence affect the team? How do people feel after interacting with you? Motivated? Stressed? Disconnected? Think back to your most recent conversations—did you come across as approachable and supportive, or were you more intense or demanding than you realized? Also consider how your vibe fits with the team's culture. Are you lifting people up, or unintentionally pushing some folks away?

- Am I empowering or micromanaging? Are you giving people real ownership, or are you stuck in the weeds of every little detail? If things only move forward when you're directly involved, it could be a sign the team's leaning on you too much—or that you're not letting go enough. True leadership means trusting others to take the lead sometimes, too.

- How do I handle feedback and mistakes? When's the last time you admitted you were wrong in front of the team? Do people feel safe giving you honest feedback—or do they tend to hold back? Pay attention to how you react in meetings. Things like defensiveness or brushing off ideas can shut down creativity and make others think twice before speaking up.

- Am I helping my team grow? Are you truly supporting your team's growth, or are you just holding on to top performers because they make you look good? Think about recent development conversations or promotions. Are you helping people move forward in their careers—or are they stuck under your leadership? Great leaders build teams that thrive even when they're not around.

- Do my values match my actions? If integrity is something you care about, are you sticking to it— even when it's hard? Think about any recent tough decisions. Did you choose what felt right for people, or just what made the most financial sense? When your actions don't reflect your values, people start to notice—and trust can take a hit.

These are just a handful of examples, but if you pause for genuine reflection, I'm confident you'll come up with some of your own. Consider the standards you hold for others. What does it look like when everything works? Then turn the lens inward: Am I truly living by those same principles?

Essential Metrics—Reflections of Your Leadership's True Influence

Although reflection offers personal insights, objective data provides an impartial perspective. These indicators serve as mirrors, revealing how your leadership style manifests in tangible outcomes. Track them consistently via HR software, performance analytics, or confidential feedback mechanisms to identify patterns in advance. Below are some examples, featuring explanations and action-oriented approaches.

Employee turnover rates: Elevated voluntary turnover, such as rates exceeding industry benchmarks, frequently indicates underlying issues with leadership effectiveness. Analyze it by department or employee tenure—for instance, if high achievers are departing, this could highlight deficiencies in acknowledgment or professional advancement.

Recommendation: Perform interviews with current employees to uncover core issues, then roll out targeted retention initiatives like structured career development, employee recognition and rewards, and ongoing training and education programs.

Exit interviews: These insights reveal honest reasons for exit, such as "insufficient support" or "toxic leadership." Recurring themes in responses expose deeper organizational flaws.

Recommendation: Strip out personal details and compile the data every three months, then address the key patterns, for instance by rolling out adaptable scheduling options to counter work-life balance concerns.

Leadership and employee engagement surveys: Tools such as 360-degree feedback or yearly surveys assess views on your leadership performance, such as ratings for trust, vision, or inclusivity. Scores under 70–80 percent on items like "My leader motivates me" signal potential gaps.

Recommendation: Disclose findings openly and develop targeted strategies, including leadership development programs, to strengthen underperforming aspects. For more information on this approach, refer to Chapter 11.

Absenteeism and sick days: Elevated rates in this area typically arise from stress or employee disengagement triggered by overly controlling management. Benchmark against industry standards—five to seven days per employee annually.

Recommendation: Launch wellness programs and monitor for burnout via regular one-on-one check-ins.

After collecting your reflections and insights, the true effort kicks in: adjustment. Develop a personal growth strategy featuring SMART (specific, measurable, achievable, relevant, and time-bound) objectives. For instance, if feedback reveals trust gaps, pledge to host biweekly candid discussions over the next half-year. Keep in mind, strong leadership is ever evolving—strategies that succeed now might fail later. Periodic self-assessments keep you aligned, helping to build teams of excellence with your direction. Through this approach, you amplify your influence while motivating those around you to reflect and advance.

3. Active Listening

The key to transforming relationships, enhancing influence, and making people feel genuinely heard is active listening. I've shared this topic with various audiences because of how widely it applies across leadership roles. It's my all-purpose leadership tool.

When you truly listen, you do more than just hear the words—you pick up on the emotions and intentions behind them. This leads people to feel valued, understood, and more willing to share their thoughts and feelings.

And the research backs this up. A 2022 survey of 443 employees from different industries in the US, published in the *Journal of Public Relations Research*, found that when employees felt like their organization and supervisors really listened to them—and communicated well overall—they reported having a stronger relationship with the organization.[1]

What's more, this connection was tied to how well their basic psychological needs were being met. When people feel heard, they're more likely to experience autonomy, competence, and a sense of connection with others—which naturally builds trust and deepens workplace relationships.

This isn't just a soft skill—not even close. It's a powerful ability that builds lasting trust, eliminates misunderstandings, and promotes meaningful conversations. Because of how essential it is, you'll see references to active listening pop up throughout this book.

Now here's how to wield this essential leadership skill.

Lock In Completely

Are you truly present and engaged with what the speaker is saying, or is your mind already jumping ahead, crafting your next clever reply? If that sounds familiar, you're not alone—it happens to many of us. In a world where distraction is the default, the ability to really listen is both uncommon and incredibly powerful.

The next time you engage in a conversation, challenge yourself to be fully present. Put away your phone, silence notifications, and give the other person your undivided attention. Resist the urge to mentally rehearse your reply while they're still speaking. I've experienced moments where someone was so fixated on delivering their comeback that they entirely missed the heart of my message, distracted by their own thoughts.

One memorable moment involved a coworker who, while incredibly sharp and quick on their feet, had a habit of planning their next response before the conversation had even finished. We were discussing a project deadline and the need to prioritize certain tasks. Midway through my point, I could see it—the spark in their eyes, already gearing up for a counterpoint. My words? Totally lost in the buildup to their reply. While it was almost impressive how ready they were, it reminded me how often we all fall into this trap—listening to respond rather than to understand.

Active listening is more than just hearing words—it's understanding the emotions, intentions, and nuances behind them. By locking in completely, you not only show respect but also deepen your connections and avoid misunderstandings. So next time, pause, breathe, and let the other person's words sink in before you respond. You might be surprised how engaging your conversations become.

Being a Conversation Partner

Think of active listening as jumping on a teeter-totter with your conversation partner—fully engaged, matching their rhythm, and syncing with their energy to make them feel like the star of the show.

Keep the positivity flowing with small cues that say, "I'm right here with you!" Nod. Say things like "Gotcha!" or "Wow, I can see that!" These simple gestures keep the mood lively and show you're truly tuned in.

Reflect their emotions. If they're buzzing with excitement, smile and match their energy. Throw in a "That's so awesome!" to keep the momentum going. If they're down or venting about a rough day, soften your tone and ground the moment with something like "Man, that sounds tough."

Want to level up? Rephrase what they said to show you're not just hearing them—you're getting them. If they're stressed, you might say, "So that surprise deadline totally threw you for a loop, huh?" That response gives a mental fist bump—*I'm with you*—without hijacking the conversation. Or if they're fired up about a new idea, respond with, "Okay, so you're saying this project is going to be a game changer. Very cool!"

Your goal is to let them know their message landed—and that you're right there with them.

And don't forget to add a little eye contact and a laugh when they crack a joke. Even a playful "No way, tell me more!" can turn a conversation into a moment they'll remember. Active listening is having your ears open and engaging your heart as well.

Dig in with Curiosity

Have you ever been in a conversation and noticed the other person's eyes glaze over, like they've mentally checked out halfway through? It's an uncomfortable moment—whether you're the one tuning out or the one being tuned out.

To avoid slipping into conversational autopilot, stay present, get curious, and explore what's really going on beneath the surface. It's in these moments that ordinary dialogue can transform into genuine connection.

Picture yourself as a dialogue detective, actively searching for context, emotion, and nuance. When something sounds vague or loaded, don't just nod and move on—pause and ask for clarification. Say something like "Wait, when you say you're swamped, is that code for inbox overflow or full-blown chaos?" By asking these clarifying questions, you keep the conversation alive and send a clear message: *I hear you, I see you, and I care enough to understand the real story.*

Curiosity fuels connection. When you bring that energy into a conversation, you turn routine exchanges into authentic ones.

Hold Your Fire

We've all been there: You're in a conversation, the wheels are turning, and you've got the perfect idea, solution, or comment ready to go. The urge to jump in is real. And hey, enthusiasm is a great thing! But sometimes, diving in too quickly can do more harm than good. I've seen it happen time and again: Someone cuts in a little too early, and suddenly, the whole flow of the conversation gets derailed. What could've been a meaningful exchange turns into a rushed or awkward back-and-forth.

So here's a simple trick: When you feel that impulse to speak, just pause. Take a breath. Tune in a little deeper to what the other person is actually saying. Let their words land before crafting your response.

And remember, those little silences or pauses in conversation are not awkward gaps you need to fill. They're valuable opportunities to demonstrate that you're truly listening. Holding back, even for a moment, shows respect, builds trust, and keeps the dialogue moving in a more thoughtful and connected way.

Respond Like a Pro

When it's your turn to respond, make every word count! Show you're tuned in to what they're saying and excited for where the conversation is headed. Consider an encouraging response like "I totally get why you see it that way!" or "Your take on this is exciting!" to align with their thoughts and build a connection. Then, share an idea to keep the energy flowing, maybe "What if we tried looking at it like this?" or "Have you thought about this angle?" If you're drawing a blank, no worries! Just smile and say, "Interesting idea—let me mull it over and come back with something." Keep an open mind, check your biases, and let your curiosity lead the way.

A touch of self-awareness and genuine curiosity can transform a simple exchange into a fantastic, meaningful conversation that leaves everyone feeling heard and inspired.

The Need to Be Heard

Let's be honest—everyone wants to feel heard. Not just nodded at or politely acknowledged, but really listened to. We crave that sense that someone's truly tuned in, not just waiting for their turn to talk. And as it turns out, this need isn't just about ego or attention—it's deeply rooted in both our evolutionary history and our biology. Science backs that up.

Back in our early human days, survival wasn't a solo act. Thriving meant being part of a tight-knit group, where communication was everything. If you spoke up and people listened, you had influence, safety, and belonging. But if you were ignored or talked over? It wasn't just annoying, it could feel like a threat. Being excluded or dismissed triggered stress responses that signaled something much deeper: possible social rejection, which in ancient times could mean actual danger.

So, we adapted. We evolved not only to communicate better, but to value being heard and understood. Neuroscience now shows that feeling heard lights up the same reward centers in the brain as receiving a gift or physical affection. It literally feels good—because it reinforces our sense of connection and psychological safety.

Anthropologist Robin Dunbar even suggests that storytelling itself evolved as a way for humans to bond. In his view, stories became a kind of verbal grooming, replacing physical grooming among larger social groups. Through shared narratives, people fostered trust, empathy, and a sense of belonging.[2]

Your Brain's in on It, Too

Modern science reveals that when someone genuinely listens to us, repeats back what we've said, asks thoughtful questions, or simply remains present, our brains light up. Dopamine, one of the four feel-good chemicals in our brains, gets released. So does oxytocin, the connection hormone that lowers stress and builds trust. That's why a good conversation can feel just as satisfying as a hug, or even a slice of your favorite pizza.

On the flip side, getting ignored or cut off lights up the amygdala, the brain's alarm system. It's the same part that kicks in when we feel threatened or anxious. That's why being brushed off in a meeting or talked over at dinner can sting more than expected; it's not just rude, it's a biological phenomenon.

So, when someone leans in and really listens, they're doing more than being polite. They're meeting a real, human need, helping us feel seen, safe, and part of something. And that's powerful.

Overcoming the Barriers

In any relationship, whether personal or professional, open and honest communication serves as the backbone for building trust, resolving conflicts, and creating mutual understanding. However, numerous barriers can hinder this vital exchange. Overcoming these barriers requires a deliberate process of self-awareness and consistent effort. Below, I'll outline some common barriers to open communication along with practical ways to address each one.

Barrier: Fear of judgment or rejection

Sometimes, we hold back from sharing our ideas or mistakes because we're afraid of being judged or rejected. This fear often comes from past experiences when opening up didn't exactly go so well—perhaps we faced criticism or felt left out. In a workplace, this can lead to playing it safe, sticking to the same old ideas, and missing out on breakthroughs. For example, you might hesitate to pitch an idea in a meeting, worried it might sound "out there," even though it could be a giant leap forward.

Strategy: Cultivate psychological safety

Psychological safety refers to a shared belief or environment in which individuals feel secure enough to take interpersonal risks, such as expressing ideas, asking questions, admitting mistakes, or voicing concerns, without fear of punishment, humiliation, embarrassment, rejection, or negative repercussions. This concept, popularized by Harvard Business School professor Amy Edmondson in the 1990s, emphasizes a culture of rewarded vulnerability that promotes open communication, collaboration, and innovation.

This approach challenges the outdated notion that leaders and teams must appear invincible. Instead, it recognizes that people thrive when they feel safe to be imperfect. Here's a practical guide to cultivating psychological safety, featuring actionable steps, tips, and methods to measure progress and achieve lasting impact.

1. Lead with your own vulnerability to break the ice: One of the most effective ways to ease the fear of judgment is to model the behavior you want to see. Start by showing a bit of your own uncertainty in everyday interactions. For instance, during a brainstorming session, you might say, "I'm not entirely sure of this plan—it feels good on paper, but I'm worried about the execution timeline. What do you think? Have I overlooked something?" But I want to be clear, the goal is not to fabricate flaws—rather, it is to *humanize* yourself as a leader or team member. By sharing your doubts authentically, you lower the barrier for others to voice theirs. Over time, this shifts the team norm from "nail it or fail it" to "let's figure this out together."

Tip: Begin small, picking one meeting per week to practice this. Track how many team members follow your lead by sharing their own hesitations, and you'll likely see an increase in participation within a few sessions.

2. Shift from critique to celebration: A common mistake in teams is the tendency to critique ideas immediately, which can leave people feeling vulnerable and defensive. Instead, shift your approach to focusing on affirmation. When someone shares an idea, respond with enthusiasm, such as "Interesting idea, thank you for bringing it up! It opens up some perspectives I hadn't thought of." This small change acknowledges the contributor first, fostering a sense of inclusion before moving to improvements. When people feel valued and heard, their confidence grows, and their imaginations flourish.

Example in action: Let's say you're part of a marketing team brainstorming a campaign. Instead of saying, "That color's off for our brand," try, "I really like the vivid feeling of that visual, great start! How could we tweak it to fit our style?" This approach results in a sense of belonging, more ideas, better collaboration, and a stronger final campaign.

3. Build trust with fun, regular check-ins: Trust grows with small, steady steps. Set up quick biweekly or monthly team check-ins (I recommend five to fifteen minutes tops) focused on how everyone's feeling, not just tasks. Ask fun, open questions, like "What's a win you're proud of this week?" or "How comfortable do you feel sharing big ideas?" Rotate who leads the conversation to keep everyone involved.

Tip: Keep it light and short to avoid it feeling like a chore. You'll be amazed at how these little moments build a tighter, more open team.

4. Foster long-term habits for sustained openness: To make openness stick, add some team rituals. Try an *idea parking lot* in meetings, where all thoughts get jotted down, no judgment, to revisit later. I have often used this drill when presenting to or training leaders, always resulting in value-added input.

Alternatively, during quarterly reviews, give recognition for a brave moment, such as when someone owned up to a mistake and it ultimately led to a win.

To see if it's working, send out a quick quarterly survey: "On a one to five scale, how safe do you feel sharing ideas or mistakes?" Look for minor improvements and tweak as needed. If things slip back, don't panic; own it and keep building that culture of openness. In just three to six months of steady effort, you'll see a team that's more open, collaborative, and creative. Feedback flows freely, silos shrink, and people feel happier, experiencing less burnout and improved retention.

Barrier: Vague communication

Have you ever sent a message like "Get this done ASAP" that left your team confused and frustrated? Vague communication occurs when your words are a bit too interpretive, incorporating terms like *soon* or *sort of* that everyone decodes differently. In the office, this can erode trust, resulting in projects that drag on forever, diminishing team spirit, and those awkward "Wait, what?" arguments. For instance, a manager's email with unclear instructions might assume shared understanding, leading to mismatched efforts and frustration. Overcoming it demands intentional strategies centered on precision and active engagement.

Strategy: Enhance clarity

To overcome vague communication, implement a structured approach that emphasizes clarity, specificity, and mutual understanding. This strategy can be applied in professional settings like teams, customer interactions, or project management. Below is a step-by-step plan.

1. Use concrete and specific language: Replace ambiguous terms with precise details. For example, instead of saying,

"Let's meet soon," specify, "Let's schedule a thirty-minute call on Thursday at 2 p.m." This minimizes room for interpretation and ensures everyone is aligned. Also, if you work with different time zones, be sure to include that as well. I have to reach back for clarification on this particular detail on a regular basis.

2. Provide sufficient context: Always include background information relevant to the message, such as why something is being requested or what the expected outcome is. This helps recipients understand the *why* behind the *what*, reducing confusion.

Poor example (lacks context): "Hey, can you update the sales report by tomorrow?"

Improved example (sufficient context): "Hi team, as we prepare for the quarterly review meeting on Friday, where we'll present key metrics to the board, I need the sales report updated with the latest Q3 data. This will help us highlight our growth trends accurately. Could you please prioritize this and have it ready for me by tomorrow morning? Thanks!"

The improved version explains the background (upcoming meeting and presentation needs), the reason for the request (to showcase growth trends), and the expected outcome (accurate highlights for the board). This reduces confusion and increases the likelihood of a timely, on-target response.

3. Practice active listening and seek clarification: When receiving a message, pause to paraphrase what you've heard (Example: "So, you're asking me to complete the report by Friday?") and ask targeted questions if anything feels unclear. This not only confirms understanding but also models clear communication for others.

4. Encourage open feedback: This builds a culture where people feel safe to point out vagueness without judgment. Regularly ask, "Is there anything I can clarify?" or "Does this make sense?"

to catch issues early and refine your approach. I have to admit, the "Does this make sense?" line is my go-to when I'm explaining pretty much anything. And let me tell you, it has served others well, as I often learn that my message needs additional detail or clarification. Does that make sense?

5. Leverage visual aids or written summaries: For complex ideas, use diagrams, bullet points, or follow-up emails to reinforce verbal discussions. This provides a tangible reference that eliminates ambiguity over time.

Call to Action

In any relationship, whether personal or professional, open and honest communication lays the foundation for genuine trust. It not only creates deeper connections but also forms the essential foundation upon which the 9 Principles of trust are built, ensuring that every interaction is grounded in authenticity and mutual respect. To help you cultivate this vital skill, below are several practical action items you can implement right away to enhance your communication habits and strengthen the trust around you.

Perform an active listening practice: Team up with a coworker for a ten-minute activity in which one individual talks uninterrupted for five minutes about a professional difficulty, as the other actively listens and then recaps the key points. Swap positions and do it again. Record what worked and what may need a little tweaking.

Share a vulnerability moment: Take a few minutes to think back on a challenging moment from your work life—maybe it was a tough project, a mistake you made, or a decision that didn't go as planned. Write a short story (about 100–200 words) about that experience. Focus on what made it difficult, what you learned from it, and how it changed the way you think or work.

Once you've written your story, share it with the team during a meeting (in person or virtual). The idea is to be genuine, to show a bit of vulnerability, and discuss how you've grown from the experience. This kind of sharing can help build trust, encourage empathy, and create space for others to open up too.

Incorporate humor in a meeting: Kick off your next team meeting on a high note by embracing some levity right from the get-go. Consider an icebreaker that gets everyone laughing and loosening up, such as kicking things off with a humorous, shareable office mishap.

I once attended a meeting where the CEO opened with: "Good morning, everyone. Before we jump in, quick story. This morning, I managed to spill coffee all over my notes. No problem, I printed a new set . . . only they're from last quarter. So, if I start celebrating Q2's numbers again, just smile and nod."

Everyone loved it!

Provide constructive feedback: In your next one-on-one or team meeting, give at least one piece of specific, kind, and direct feedback to a colleague, focusing on actionable improvement, such as: "I noticed your presentation was clear. Adding visuals could make it even more engaging."

Reflect on communication styles: Take fifteen minutes to reflect, and jot down some thoughts about how you communicate with your team. Think about how you share info, give feedback, or listen during conversations. Try to identify one thing you could do better. Maybe it's being clearer in your messages, using a more thoughtful tone, or really tuning in when others are speaking. Once you've pinpointed something, set a simple, realistic goal to work on that area over the next week.

"No journey toward excellence is a solo mission. To truly move forward and stay ahead, you need an inspired crew at your side."

NOTES

NOTES

CHAPTER TWO: THE 2ND PRINCIPLE

FULFILLING COMMITMENTS

The Impact of Small Promises

Oh, if only I could hop into a time machine and zip back to patch up those little cracks in trust before they turned into canyons! My mission now is to treat every commitment, no matter how small, as if it's the crown jewel of my day. It may be tough to imagine, but there's this strange truth: The smallest promises, those little "Sure thing!" moments we throw around so casually, pack the biggest punch. They can either chip away at trust or build it into something rock-solid and beautiful.

It was one of those hectic office days when your inbox feels like the universe's practical joke and the phone rings like it's out for revenge. Amid the turmoil, my teammate Lidia dropped by with a hopeful glance. She was grappling with the new HRIS (human resource information system, a big name with a bigger hassle) and wanted a quick review of recent training. "I'm all yours!" I said, my optimism gleaming. At that moment, I was fully committed.

But, oh boy, the day sure had other plans! Meetings stacked up, deadlines loomed, and before I knew it, that cheerful *absolutely* morphed into a silent *absolutely not*. It's not like I meant to ditch Lidia, honestly! It's just that the day got away from me. To make matters worse, I didn't even send her a quick "Hey, can we hit pause and reschedule?" That tiny gesture, barely a blip in my day, could've been a sign flashing: *I care about you and your needs!* Instead, my silence sent a different message that chipped away at the trust I didn't even realize was at stake.

Fast-forward a few weeks, and I discovered Lidia had sorted out the training independently. *Awesome, she's so resourceful!* I thought, giving myself a mental high five. However, I then noticed something was off. Lidia wasn't her usual positive self. The easy chats we often shared had been replaced by polite nods and a subtle distance, as if she had built an invisible wall. Curiosity got the better of me, so I finally asked her what was up. And, well, she laid it on me! That little broken promise, which felt relatively insignificant to me, had a much bigger impact on her. It wasn't just the training—it was feeling valued, seen, and respected. My heart sank as I realized how one minor oversight could have such a profound impact.

Restoring that trust wasn't simple—it required dedicated effort. I prioritized connecting with Lidia regularly, not just regarding tasks but also about her thoughts and daily life. I honored every commitment, no matter how small, whether it was a quick chat or approving a time off request by noon. Gradually, those consistent, small gestures began to heal the damage. Lidia's usual upbeat self returned, and our conversations felt like they used to.

Through it all, I learned something valuable: Those small commitments aren't just tasks to manage. They're the glue that holds relationships together, helps teams excel, and builds trust. So, here's my new mantra: No promise is too small to keep, and no moment is too busy to show someone they matter. Who knew the tiniest "I've got you" could mean so much?

The second principle is the ultimate trait of a great leader who keeps promises, like a friend who always shows up when they say they will.

This principle extends beyond simply keeping your word—it fosters an environment of trust and reliability that makes your team, clients, and partners feel confident they're in good hands. When you deliver on promises, big or small, you enable smoother collaboration, boost team spirit, and inspire everyone about the mission. But if you drop the ball, even by accident, it's like forgetting to show up one too many times—people start to wonder if you're really all in.

This is leading by example: demonstrating to your team that your words carry weight, supported by action and a clear strategy. Below, we'll explore how to establish this principle as a foundation for your leadership, ensuring consistency while staying genuine and approachable.

1. Align Promises with Organizational Goals

When it comes to making promises, they need to be realistic, but you also need to ensure that your commitments align with the bigger picture. As a leader, you should outline promises that are achievable and aligned with the organization's strategic goals. You need to concentrate on initiatives that have a significant impact, those that drive the company's vision forward without overloading the team. Even your small, casual promises may require prioritization and consideration of their impact and feasibility. Sometimes, you may have to muster the courage to say no to alluring but impractical ideas, even if they sound exciting. And when this happens, be sure to embrace open and honest communication!

The Misaligned Promise

Jersey Boy Snacks was a mid-sized food manufacturing company known for its quirky, artisanal potato chips and granola bars. Leading the charge was CEO Tim Shapley, an upbeat foodie whose love for his team was matched only by his dream of seeing Jersey Boy Snacks in every pantry across America. Tim was admired by his employees, always ready with a high five and a talent for rallying everyone with tales of glory.

Two years ago, at a company-wide meeting, Tim stood before his 200 employees, a bag of barbecue chips in hand, and proclaimed with a grin, "Listen up folks! Within a year, you'll all have free snacks at your desks, a four-day workweek, and a 15 percent raise!" The crowd cheered, already dreaming of longer weekends and endless munchies.

Behind the scenes, however, Jersey Boy's board and executives were devising a different strategy: a major effort to enter national grocery chains. The company was investing heavily in new packaging machines, organic ingredient suppliers, and an advertising campaign. These actions were vital to competing with snack giants, but they left little for Tim's employee perks.

Tim's promises came from the heart—he was convinced that happy workers would improve morale and performance. However, he hadn't thoroughly checked in with the board or discussed the budget with the CFO, who warned him that the company's funds were thin. Tim brushed off the concerns, confident he could persuade investors to fund the expansion and his employee perks.

Months passed, and employees started asking about their raises and snack stashes. Tim dished out replies, mentioning minor hiccups due to big growth plans. Meanwhile, the board was getting restless. They argued Tim's promises didn't match the priority of landing shelf space at major retailers. A four-day workweek could disrupt production schedules, and raises would erode funds for new equipment.

Things got dicey at the next annual meeting. Expecting news on their perks, employees got a presentation about Jersey Boy's new vegan granola line and a viral TikTok campaign. The mood plummeted. One packing line supervisor, David, stood up and asked, "Yo, Tim, what's up with the raises and free snacks you discussed?" The room went quiet. Tim, caught off guard, mumbled about tight budgets and needing to grow the brand first.

The crunch was real. Trust in Tim took a hit. David and a few coworkers jumped ship to a rival snack company with better hours. Online, anonymous employee posts popped up, calling Tim's leadership "all flavor, no follow-through."

Tim was devastated. He hadn't meant to make unrealistic promises—he truly believed he could deliver. The board, still fond of his enthusiasm, insisted on leadership coaching. Over the next year, Tim worked to rebuild trust. He hosted an open forum called Chips & Chats, accepting his mistake and laying out a practical plan for smaller perks, like monthly snack boxes and a hybrid work option, that fit the company's budget.

By the following year, Jersey Boy Snacks was back in its rhythm. A deal with a major supermarket chain was finalized, and Tim's reduced perks were implemented seamlessly. Employees appreciated his honesty, even though some still yearned for that four-day week. Tim learned a valuable lesson: Even the crunch-iest promises must be baked with a solid plan and aligned with the company's core recipe.

Unpacking Tim's Promise

I've navigated a situation strikingly similar to the one Tim recently encountered. It was a challenging and often turbulent experience that tested my resilience and decision-making skills. Yet, it also became a profound learning opportunity, shaping my perspective on leadership, accountability, and trust. Below, I'll delve into the specifics of Tim's off-target promise, analyze the missteps that led to its unraveling, and offer practical, actionable strategies to ensure commitments align with organizational goals while building trust with stakeholders.

Conduct a Feasibility Check

Before making bold promises that aim to inspire and motivate, ensure that your team has the necessary resources, time, and priorities to deliver on those commitments. Evaluate whether your budget, personnel, and tools can realistically support your ambitious plans and ensure successful execution.

For example, Tim could have avoided overpromising by tak-ing a few minutes to speak informally with the CFO and verify the availability of funds for proposed raises, bonuses, or perks—before rallying the team with enthusiasm. By doing this quick reality check, he would have grounded his promises and protected his credibility.

When you plan thoughtfully and act with accountability, you build trust with your team and stakeholders. This intentional approach aligns expectations, prevents setbacks, and makes your vision both inspiring and achievable—laying the foundation for sustainable success.

Plan with a Clear Roadmap

To achieve success, turn commitments into a structured plan by breaking them down into actionable, well-defined steps. Develop a detailed roadmap that includes specific timelines, allocated budgets, and clearly assigned responsibilities to ensure steady progress. Involve your team in the planning process to inspire ownership and clarity. Schedule regular check-ins to monitor milestones, evaluate progress, address any roadblocks, and maintain alignment with the overarching goals. Stay flexible and ready to adjust the plan as challenges arise or new opportunities emerge, ensuring the project stays on track without losing sight of the ultimate goal.

For example, consider Tim's second approach: He excelled by designing a *realistic* perk plan that not only aligned with the company's financial objectives but also prioritized employee motivation and engagement. By establishing clear milestones, assigning tasks to the right team members, and regularly reviewing progress, Tim ensured the plan was executed effectively. His proactive adjustments to the timeline and budget, based on team feedback and financial updates, kept the project aligned with both short-term needs and long-term company goals, ultimately driving success and boosting team morale.

Share Openly and Keep Everyone in the Loop

When you face a challenge, setback, or delay, take charge—don't let ambiguity lead to confusion. Be proactive and transparent.

Clearly explain what's happening and why, and outline a concrete plan to move forward. Open, honest communication builds trust and keeps everyone aligned.

For example, instead of giving vague updates like Tim's "minor hiccups," which frustrated and confused the team, offer a detailed explanation of the issue, its impact, and the next steps. This approach fosters clarity and maintains confidence.

To keep everyone informed, build consistent communication habits. Schedule regular check-ins—such as weekly team meetings, brief progress reports, or friendly email updates—to sustain momentum and quickly address questions. These touchpoints prevent misunderstandings and ensure everyone stays in the loop.

By prioritizing clear, timely, and inclusive communication, you foster a collaborative environment where trust thrives and teams stay united—ready to overcome challenges together.

Own Mistakes and Rebuild Trust

Look, we all stumble from time to time. Perfection is a myth, and pretending otherwise helps no one. What does help is owning your missteps with sincerity, humility, and a proactive mindset. When things go sideways, resist the urge to deflect or downplay. Instead, take the courageous route: Acknowledge the mistake clearly, explain what happened without excuses, and share how you plan to make it right.

This kind of transparency shows integrity and earns respect. People don't expect you to be flawless—they expect you to be real. When you're open about a mistake, take responsibility, and follow through with meaningful action, you're doing more than fixing a problem; you're rebuilding trust and reinforcing a culture where accountability and growth matter. That kind of openness builds a bridge of authenticity with your team, customers, or partners. It shows that you're committed to learning, keeping your promises, and doing right by those who rely on you.

Vulnerability paired with action is powerful—it proves you're human, relatable, and genuinely invested. And that's not just good leadership, it's how trust is earned and sustained.

2. Clarify Expectations

Let's say you're a leader ready to make a significant promise— maybe it's delivering a project, boosting team morale with free lunch Fridays, or ensuring everyone gets a floating holiday for working a specified amount of overtime. But before you seal the deal with a hearty handshake, you've got to make sure everyone's on the same page. That's where clarifying expectations comes in.

Suppose you promise your team "an awesome workplace." It sounds like a total win, right? But while you're picturing a shiny new coffee maker, your team is imagining four-day workweeks or a foosball table straight out of a tech startup fantasy. Without clarity, you set the stage for a comedy of errors, disappointed faces, and confused shrugs. Clarifying expectations ensures everyone knows what's being promised, how it'll happen, and what success looks like.

The SMART Method: Perfecting Promises

To ensure clarity, borrow a page from the SMART playbook: specific, measurable, achievable, relevant, and time-bound.[3] It's like a recipe for a promise that is clear and achievable. Let's break it down with a fun example: promising your team a revamped break room.

Specific: Don't just say, "We'll improve the break room." Spell it out! "We'll add a cozy couch, a mini fridge stocked with sodas, and some wall art to make the break room a hangout spot." Now everyone's picturing the same thing.

Measurable: How will you know you've nailed it? "We'll survey the team two weeks after the upgrade to ensure 80 percent of you love the new setup." Numbers keep it real.

Achievable: Be adventurous, but realistic. A couch and fridge? Doable. A full-on arcade with a claw machine? Maybe pump the brakes unless your budget is limitless.

Relevant: Does this promise matter to your team? A cool break room is spot-on if they're begging for a place to unwind. If they're more concerned about their workload, consider hiring extra support staff.

Time-bound: Set a deadline to keep things moving. "We'll have the break room ready by the end of next month." No one likes a promise that drags on.

Using the SMART framework is like installing sturdy guard-rails on your promise, ensuring it stays on track and doesn't derail. It sets clear boundaries, aligning everyone with a shared sense of purpose and preventing the goal from drifting into vague, wishy-washy territory where confusion and missteps can derail progress and dilute accountability.

3. Follow Through Relentlessly

Make promises nonnegotiable. When you commit, it's your chance to stand out! Treating promises as nonnegotiable shows that you're not just talking the talk. People will start to see you as reliable. Relentless follow-through builds trust and makes you the go-to person for getting things done. Life loves to throw curveballs: traffic jams, surprise meetings, or a sudden call from your ex. But relentless follow-through means you don't let those hiccups derail you. Obstacles? What obstacles? If you promised to finish that project by 5 p.m., you're working on it even if your office buddy tempts you to ditch early for a round of drinks. To make the most of it, invite them to lend a hand, and you can both head out to celebrate once it's done.

Following through isn't always a matter of grand promises. Sometimes it's the little things, like replying to a text, completing a task, or taking care of the plants you promised not to let die (again). These small victories accumulate, boosting your confidence and making you feel like you could conquer anything. Treat promises as if they're carved in stone. When you do, it becomes contagious. Your team will begin to adopt your reliability habits. Before you know it, your team is crushing deadlines and showing up on time, all because you set the pace. And, if you happen to misstep, don't spiral into a guilt-fest. Brush yourself off, apologize if needed, and get back on the promise-keeping train.

The Caveat

Okay, reality check: It's important to recognize that preserving trust doesn't always mean you have to follow through on every single promise, no matter what. Life happens, priorities shift, and sometimes things just aren't possible anymore. Maybe an urgent issue comes up, your resources change, or new information forces you to rethink your original plan. In these moments, sticking to your word for the sake of it can actually backfire—so some flexibility is not just acceptable, it's necessary.

But here's the crucial part: How you handle the change matters more than the change itself. Open, honest communication is everything. Don't just break the news last minute and disappear—let people know as soon as possible what's happening, and, just as importantly, share the reasons behind it. When you explain the why, you show respect and keep everyone in the loop, which goes a long way toward maintaining trust, even if the message is disappointing.

Always approach these conversations with genuine empathy and humility. Acknowledge any inconvenience or frustration your change might cause and show that you understand how it affects those involved. Tone matters, too—avoid sounding dismissive, defensive, or detached.

And this is a big one: Don't play the blame game. It's tempting to deflect responsibility—maybe by saying, "This was corporate's decision," or "Upper management forced my hand." But in the long run, those explanations just make you look like you're dodging accountability, and people notice. It erodes trust and undermines your credibility as a leader. Instead, stick to the objective facts, take ownership for what you can, and be transparent about the factors that led to the decision—without name-dropping or making scapegoats out of others. It's always better to focus on the situation than to point fingers.

In short, maintaining trust doesn't mean being inflexible; it means handling changes openly, responsibly, and with respect for everyone involved.

Overcoming the Barriers

Keeping promises is the foundation of trust and credibility. Yet even the most well-intentioned leaders often hit unexpected roadblocks that can make follow-through feel like an uphill battle. These hurdles, whether internal doubts or external pressures, risk eroding team morale and long-term relationships if left unchecked. Below, we'll explore some key barriers and straight-forward ways to navigate them.

Barrier: Unforeseen external disruptions

Surprise curveballs from the outside can throw a real wrench in your business plans and progress. Sudden economic hiccups, supply chain snags, geopolitical drama, Mother Nature's disruptions, or global health scares can upend even the best-laid strategies in an instant. Hitting you out of nowhere, they affect everything from production to shipping and sales, making it more challenging than ever to keep those promises on track.

Strategy: Foster resilience against disruptions

Build resilience by creating adaptive systems that absorb shocks, minimize downtime, and enable swift recovery. This proactive mindset shifts businesses from reactive firefighting to strategic agility, turning potential threats into opportunities for innovation and efficiency.

Here are a few considerations:

- **Scenario planning and risk assessment:** Think ahead by running through what-if situations before they happen. Get folks from different teams together to talk through possible bumps in the road like market shifts, new rules, or tech changes, and see how your current plans hold up. It's a great way to spot weak spots early and stay ready for whatever comes next.

- **Diversify supply chains:** Don't put all your eggs in one basket. Spread out your suppliers across different regions so you're not stuck if something goes wrong. Line up a couple of backups, keep an eye on performance (AI tools can help), and make sure your contracts give you room to adjust if things get messy.

- **Build buffers:** Give yourself some wiggle room. Add 10–20 percent extra time to projects, keep a small stockpile of key supplies (one to three months' worth), and always have a backup plan. Whether it's extra hands or extra gear, a little prep now saves a lot of stress later.

Barrier: Fear of disappointing

The pressure to keep everyone happy—your team, your boss, your family—can be overwhelming, especially when the costs are high and your decisions really matter. That pressure often shows up as hesitation to make significant moves, holding back from delegating, second-guessing every email or conversation, and struggling to follow through on commitments. At the root of it all? A fear of letting people down, being criticized, or just plain failing.

Sometimes, that fear comes from past career stumbles that still sting, a perfectionist streak built over years of chasing success, or company cultures that treat mistakes like the end of the world.

If left unchecked, this kind of mindset can slowly erode your confidence. It can lead to burnout or even impostor syndrome, where despite promotions, praise, or big wins, you still feel like you don't belong. You tell yourself you just got lucky, or that you've fooled everyone into thinking you're better than you are. And this doesn't just affect you. That kind of energy spreads.

Teams can pick up on the tension, and it can cause them to play it safe, stay quiet, or avoid bringing new ideas to the table, worried they might mess up or make things worse.

The good news? You can break out of this pattern. Here are a few ways to start turning things around.

Strategy: Attack fear head-on

Fear of letting people down is an unfortunate trap, especially in leadership roles. However, you can tackle it with simple habits that build courage, revise your thinking, and strengthen your team. Here's a guide with easy steps.

1. Realize and confront your fear: Spot the root cause so it doesn't sneak up and catch you off guard.

- **Fear audit:** On a weekly basis, take fifteen minutes to write down decisions where doubt hits. Ask: What's the worst I'm imagining? Real proof or old ghosts? Spot patterns like perfectionism to loosen its hold.

- **Flip the script:** Swap "I can't mess up" for "Growth beats perfect, bumps are short, wins last." Use value-based mantras like "Leading real, not flawless" to shift from a negative to a positive mindset.

- **Get outside input:** Chat with a mentor about a nagging choice. Their take often reveals that the risks aren't as huge as they feel, making it seem normal.

2. Sharpen choices and delegation: Kick hesitation by trusting action and sharing the load.

- **Improve decision-making:** For tough calls, create a pros/cons list, then sleep on it for twenty-four hours. This turns worry into smart moves without holding you back.

- **Delegate easy first:** Pick low-risk stuff (like reports) and say, "You're owning this, I trust your skills." Follow with cheers, not hovering, to share the weight and show it's okay to lean on the team.

- **Set reasonable goals:** Set clear wins up front, "80 percent on time works for now." Ditch perfection to celebrate progress and ditch the dread of critics. In time, you'll be able to confidently elevate your expectations and goals.

3. Promote openness and team energy: Streamlined conversations ease stress and ignite the imagination.

- **Be transparent:** In meetings, say, "I'm contemplating this because I care about us. What do you think?" It settles the pressure, invites input, and shows flaws are fine.

- **Make feedback fun:** Do quick shout-out circles for wins and tips. Share your own old flop and how it helped. This builds a safe space where feedback fuels growth, not fear.

- **Draw boundaries:** With bosses or family, try "I'm all in here, but I need time to focus if I'm going to nail it." This keeps you from burning out without compromising your commitment.

4. Keep the momentum going: Lock in habits to dodge burnout or doubt.

- **Self-care:** Stick to walks or ten-minute breathing sessions daily. Notice how it calms the jitters. A calm body leads to a steady mind.

- **Celebrate small wins:** When you end a week with a fear-beating moment, treat yourself to something grand, or perhaps just a fancy coffee. Rewarding yourself in this way trains your brain to expect confidence boosts.

- **Check in every three months:** Flip through notes or talk with a mentor or friend. Have you noticed less stalling? Is your team exhibiting courage? Are you fulfilling your commitments? Assess and revise as necessary.

Call to Action

Consistently honoring your commitments is paramount to building trust, reliability, and strong relationships with your team, colleagues, and partners. When you reliably follow through on your promises, you demonstrate integrity and dependability, building confidence in your ability to deliver. This not only strengthens professional bonds but also enhances your reputation as a trustworthy individual. To help you maintain this level of accountability and ensure you meet your obligations, here are some actionable steps to guide you in following through on your commitments.

Create a basic feasibility assessment: Before making major commitments or sharing plans with your team, begin with a small-scale commitment. Arrange a short feasibility review meeting with key stakeholders (such as finance, HR, or project leaders) and inform them that this step will be integrated into the process. Once you and the team are comfortable with this approach, you can proceed to larger, more complex commitments.

Create a SMART goal: To build a habit of using SMART goals to meet your commitments, begin today by selecting a straightforward goal, like a simple promise, and creating a SMART worksheet. Examine the goal to confirm it aligns with each criteria: specific, measurable, achievable, relevant, and time-bound. With practice, this process will become second nature, and you won't need a worksheet.

Prioritize and organize: Try starting your day tomorrow by creating a to-do list to track your commitments, prioritizing tasks based on urgency and importance. This will help you stay focused and ensure nothing slips through the cracks. I have been starting every day with a to-do list for over 20 years. Yes, even on weekends, although I suppose that's more of a *honey-do* list.

*"Vulnerability paired with action is powerful—
it proves you're human, relatable, and
genuinely invested. And that's not just good
leadership—it's how trust is
earned and sustained."*

NOTES

NOTES

CHAPTER THREE: THE 3RD PRINCIPLE

APPROACHABILITY

The Power of Approachable Leadership

I wish I had a dollar for every time I've heard from frustrated leaders who are dismayed to learn that their team members are bypassing them to seek guidance from, ask questions of, or voice concerns to another leader, often someone outside their department or chain of command. Time and again, this issue boils down to the same root cause: The leader in question struggles to cultivate an approachable presence, which undermines trust and open communication within their team. This lack of approachability often leaves subordinates feeling hesitant to engage directly, pushing them to seek support elsewhere.

Outstanding leadership demands far more than simply steering the ship through turbulent storms or charting ambitious new courses. It calls for a deeper, more profound skill: the ability to connect with people on a genuine heartfelt level, one that feels truly authentic, infused with kindness, and profoundly human. At its core, being an approachable leader is an essential foundation for forging lasting relationships, cultivating trust, and inspiring teams to achieve extraordinary things together.

Early in my career, I got a front-row ticket to a lesson in how *not* to lead. My manager back then was like a walking Keep Out sign. Picture a guy whose face seemed locked into a permanent display of disappointment, as if smiling might cause a full system crash. His entire essence screamed all work and no fun, with a leadership style taken straight from a 1980s corporate handbook: top-down, no chit-chat, and no laughs. His office door? Always shut, both literally and figuratively. Walking in felt like stepping into a principal's office for a reprimand. Meetings were stiff, tensions were high, and good luck trying to toss out a new idea, ask a question, or God forbid, admit to a mistake without bracing for a full nuclear impact.

The fallout was predictable yet brutal. Over the course of several months, trust eroded, team engagement plummeted, and great ideas vanished like toilet paper during a pandemic. We all operated like drones on autopilot, simply trying to survive until the clock hit 5 p.m. People stopped caring about the work because they didn't feel valued as individuals. It was a textbook case of a leader so emotionally distant that the entire team mentally clocked out, counting down the minutes until they could escape the stifling atmosphere.

Then, like a beam of sunlight piercing through a stormy sky (cue the heavenly angel music), I caught a glimpse of what authentic leadership could look like in another department.

Enter Jackie, a manager who was the polar opposite of Captain Catastrophe, a kind, approachable beacon in the corporate wilderness. Jackie didn't just lead—she connected. She'd stroll into the office with a genuine smile, her energy inviting. She'd ask her team about their weekend concerts, kids' sporting events, or what they thought of the latest twist in their favorite Netflix series. It wasn't some staged, overly rehearsed act—Jackie was simply that person who made you feel genuinely noticed and understood. Whether someone was tossing out a fearless, off-the-wall idea or ranting about a project driving them up the wall, she'd listen fully, without judgment, without interrupting, just complete, sincere focus.

That openness was inspiring. It transformed her team's dynamic into something inspiring. People felt safe to brainstorm without fear of looking foolish, safe to take risks without worrying about a slap on the wrist, and safe to fail because they knew Jackie had their backs. The result? Trust escalated, ideas flowed, and the team didn't just get the job done—they crushed it! They collaborated enthusiastically, supported one another, and produced innovative and downright impressive work. Meetings felt like creative think tanks rather than interrogations. People didn't just show up to work—they brought their whole selves, quirks and all, because Jackie made it clear they were valued as humans, not just cogs in a machine.

Years later, I still think of Jackie with awe and gratitude. The lessons I learned from Jackie are etched in my mind, and I have carried them with me ever since: Approachability is a must-have skill that separates the truly great from the merely good. When you let your human side show, you don't just chip away at barriers—you destroy them.

The third principle is where approachable leadership shines, blending compassion, trust, and connection to make everyone feel at home. This doesn't mean you have to be the coolest boss ever—it's more focused on creating an environment where your team can share innovative ideas, voice their concerns, and bring their authentic selves to work.

The ability lies in positive appeal, a blend of how you speak, show up, and carry yourself. It requires a focus on being authentic, upbeat, and honest—someone your team wants to spend quality time with. However, before we dive in to the key elements of this principle, I feel it is prudent to explain why adopting a positive demeanor requires considerable effort. It sounds odd, but negativity often feels easier, doesn't it?

Here's why: Our brains are wired with something referred to today as negativity bias, a survival mechanism from thousands of years ago when humans faced constant threats like predators, rival groups, or scarce resources. This bias made our ancestors hyper-aware of dangers to survival. For instance, a rustle in the bushes might signal a predator, so the brain prioritized rapid responses to potential threats over enjoying a meal. One bad experience with a toxic plant could be deadly, so negative memories were etched deeply to prevent recurrence. Social rejection could lead to isolation and death, making humans highly sensitive to criticism or exclusion. This negativity bias gave adverse events more urgency and lasting impact, with the brain dedicating more resources to processing threats than positive moments.

Although we no longer dodge predators, this bias persists, shaping how we process information, make decisions, and interact. Positivity, while valuable for broadening perspectives and building resilience, lacks the same evolutionary urgency, making it harder to sustain without conscious effort.

Now, let's explore a few exciting and fun components of this leadership principle and how to blend them effectively.

1. Positive Speaking: Words That Ignite Connection

There's an adage I love to quote: "The words we speak become the house we live in." Think about that for a second: Your words aren't just fleeting sounds or scribbled notes—they're the very foundation of the environment you create and the legacy you leave. As a leader, your words are the soundtrack of your influence. Choose the right tune, and you'll have everyone, from colleagues and teams to customers, moving to the same beat, energized and united. Pick the wrong one, and you're left with a silent room or a discordant mess.

Positive speaking isn't just plastering a fake grin on every sentence, sugarcoating difficult truths, or avoiding challenges. It means wielding your words with intention, crafting messages that create joy, collaboration, and 100 percent authenticity. You exude verbal positivity, uplifting and impossible to ignore. When you speak with positivity, you're not merely communicating—you're building bridges, igniting inspiration, and creating a space where ideas flourish and people feel recognized.

Here's how to master the art of being positive and making every word count.

Clarity and Encouragement

As a leader, your words can energize your team by enhancing their motivation and focus through clear, warm communication that acknowledges challenges and inspires action. For example, if a project feels like a mountain, try saying, "Wow, this project's a big one, right? It's intense, but I'm seriously impressed by the ideas and hustle you're bringing. Let's grab lunch and figure out the next steps together. What's your top priority?" This validates the difficulty while developing trust and teamwork, demonstrating that you're fully committed to their success.

When mistakes happen (and they totally will), don't jump to critique or grill them with "What went wrong?" That can erode confidence. Instead, maintain a kind and collaborative approach. If someone bombs a presentation, say, "Oof, we've all had those off days, I've been there! Let's make the next one better. What do you think tripped you up, and how can we prepare better for round two?" This turns a fumble into a growth moment while keeping the conversation positive.

Now, don't just focus on fixing what's broken; actively seek out what's working. Make it your mission to spot and recognize excellence in real time. And don't overlook your top performers just because they're consistently delivering. This is one of the most common errors I see leaders make. Your A players also need to feel seen. Recognize and credit the person who shows up strong, drives results, and keeps the momentum going behind the scenes.

Stay engaged and present, with a positive tone and body language. When you witness great work, call it out with specific, timely praise. Ditch the generic "nice job" and say exactly what impressed you and why it matters. Try something like: "The way you handled that client objection today was sharp, you kept the conversation moving, and shifted the energy entirely. That's leadership in action."

Make recognition the norm, not the afterthought. Call out what's going right, and you'll reinforce the behaviors and mindsets you want more of. You'll energize your team to keep pushing forward and raising the bar.

Celebrate wins as they happen. Show your team what success looks like, and you'll build a culture rooted in appreciation, motivation, and continuous growth. Recognition isn't fluff—it's fuel. And when you deliver it with authenticity, it becomes one of the most powerful tools in your leadership toolkit.

At its core, clear, positive, and uplifting communication creates an environment where people feel seen, valued, and ready to show up. When you choose your words intentionally and keep the dialogue open, you build a team that's connected, resilient, and motivated to take on whatever comes next—together.

Tone and Delivery

Your tone is like the perfect blend of spice in a recipe: Get it just right, and it's a crowd-pleaser; too flat, and it's forgettable; too sharp, and it leaves a sour aftertaste. A warm, steady tone sends a message: *I'm here, I'm listening, and I genuinely care.*

My wife, an exceptional surgical nurse with a gift for connecting with people, has shared countless stories about her patients, many of whom arrive filled with anxiety and uncertainty. She explains how she intentionally adopts a soothing, reassuring tone that gently eases their fears, helping them feel calm and confident that they're in capable hands. It's not just the words she chooses—it's the way they envelop the listener, like a comforting embrace, that makes all the difference.

Now, let's take it to the next level and lean in to active listening. Show that you're tuned in with a nod, a thoughtful tilt of the head, or a quick paraphrase like "So, what I'm hearing is . . . " It's like tossing a conversational ball back and forth—it keeps things flowing and demonstrates your engagement.

Maintain a friendly and approachable tone, even when delivering tough feedback or navigating tricky moments. A light touch, perhaps with a hint of humor when appropriate, can transform a tense exchange into something that feels human and collaborative.

Dodge the Negativity Trap

Let's face it: It's incredibly easy to fall into the quicksand of negativity when things go wrong. You know, those condescending, blame-loaded comments like "Seriously, why is this late again?" or "What's the holdup this time?" They might feel satisfying in the moment, but they're nothing short of a team morale trainwreck. Instead, try flipping the script with something like "Hey, let's dig into what's slowing us down and see how we can team up to fix it."

I once worked with a leader who was an absolute expert in this area. Her name was Paula. Picture this: When a project deadline was missed, instead of dishing out eye rolls or passive-aggressive emails, Paula would call a quick team huddle with a grin and say, "All right, folks, life's messy sometimes! What's the bottleneck here, and how do we kick it out of the way for next time?" Pointing fingers and placing blame weren't part of the equation—it was rallying everyone to solve the puzzle together. The result? The team didn't feel dragged down or disciplined—they felt supported, energized, and ready to tackle the next challenge.

This approach maintains a light mood, supports collaboration, and turns setbacks into opportunities for growth. So, the next time you feel tempted to resort to sarcasm or blame, take a lesson from Paula and breathe deeply, channel that positive energy, and observe how it transforms the room. You've got this!

Quick tip: Before you let those words fly, take a moment and ask yourself, *Is this going to build a connection or slam the door on one?* That tiny pause can work wonders, transforming a snap judgment or critique into an engaging conversation starter that invites real dialogue.

2. Positive Appearance: Look Like You're Ready to Connect

Your appearance is much more than just your outfit or how you carry yourself—it's your demeanor's grand opening, your personal billboard screaming, *Hey there! I'm ready to lead, connect, and maybe even grab lunch*. It's all in crafting a look and energy that communicates, *I'm approachable, trustworthy, and totally in the game*. When you nail this, you're not just showing up—you're inviting trust, promoting collaboration, and making people think, *I need to chat with this person in the hallway ASAP*. Ready to make that first positive impression? Let's dive in to the details and break it down!

Professionalism with Personality

Your look is your personal logo, your brand if you will. So, make it stand out without shouting. Dressing professionally doesn't mean morphing into a corporate robot or strutting in runway couture. It's aligning with the culture of your workplace while adding in a dash of your authentic self. If you're in a laid-back tech startup, ditch the stiff suit for a crisp blazer, tailored jeans, and sneakers that say, *I'm cool but still mean business*. In a buttoned-up corporate office? Go classic with a sharp suit or dress, but add a quirky tie, a colorful scarf, or even a lapel pin that elicits a chuckle.

I once worked with a team manager who always wore colorful socks featuring polka dots and cartoon characters. I even spotted him wearing glowing planets one day—hilarious! It was subtle, but his unspoken message was clear: *I'm genuine and confident in my style*. The trick? Find that sweet spot where you respect the workplace but let your personality peek through. When your team sees you owning your style, it permits them to do the same.

Body Language

I'm an unapologetic people watcher, and I'm not even a little bit sorry! There's something endlessly fascinating about observing how folks move through the world. It's like being a detective of human behavior, piecing together clues from how someone strides across a room, plops into a chair, chats with a barista, or navigates a crowded party. And let me be clear: This isn't passing judgment or sizing people up—it's appreciating the unspoken stories we all tell through our quirks and gestures.

Have you ever noticed how some people just own a space the moment they walk in? It's not sorcery—it's their energy, their presence. That's body language at work, and it's doing most of the talking. Experts say that up to 70 percent of communication is nonverbal before you even say hello. I like to think of it as your personal choreography, especially if you're leading a team or trying to make an impression. You stroll into a meeting with a genuine smile that crinkles your eyes and steady eye contact that says, I see you. It's like rolling out a red carpet for a positive connection. It screams, *I'm here, I'm ready, let's make something happen!*

And then there's the subtle stuff that packs a punch. Leaning in just a smidge when someone's pitching an idea? That's the nonverbal equivalent of a "Heck yeah, I'm with you!" It shows you're locked in. A relaxed posture, a well-timed nod, or even the way you tilt your head while listening can transform a conversation into a moment of genuine connection. These little moves are like unlocking the mysteries of charisma—they make people feel heard and valued without you saying a word.

But, oh boy, the flip side can be a real disaster. Ever watch someone flop onto a couch like a deflated beach ball? Or maybe they're glaring at the wall, arms folded tighter than a sealed vault, or scrolling through their phone while someone's pouring their heart out. It's disengaged and practically shouting, *I'd rather be anywhere but here*. And the worst part is that most people don't even realize they're sending these signals. Body language is like a Wi-Fi signal—you're constantly broadcasting, whether you mean to or not.

So, next time you're out among others, have some fun with it. Play around with your own nonverbal cues. Stand a little taller, uncross those arms, and flash a smile that says, *I'm stoked to be here*. Watch how it shifts the energy in the room. And while you're at it, keep an eye on the people around you, not to judge but to marvel at the silent symphony of human behavior we're all conducting every day.

Demeanor Matters

Own the energy you bring into the room. Your demeanor isn't just how people see or hear you—it's how they *feel* connected to you. Leadership isn't about being the loudest voice or the flashiest presence; it's about showing up with calm confidence that says, *I've got this, and we're in it together.*

Your presence should be real, grounded, and uplifting. Bring warmth into every space you enter and let people know they're seen, heard, and valued. It's not just about posture or tone—it's about the emotional current you create in every conversation. That energy builds trust, sparks collaboration, and turns ordinary moments into meaningful ones.

Make people feel good about working with you—not because you're perfect, but because you're *present*. Be the kind of leader who makes others feel safe, appreciated, and energized. The one who lifts the mood in the room—not with ego, but with genuine intention.

Think back to a coach, teacher, or mentor who made you believe you could take on anything—and enjoy it. Channel that same energy. Be confident without being intimidating, polished without being distant, and real without trying too hard. That's the kind of presence that builds loyal teams, strong partnerships, and lasting influence.

If you're more on the quiet or introverted side, that's not a weakness—it's a strength. You don't need to be loud to make an impact. Be intentional about your energy. Before stepping into a meeting, take a breath and remind yourself: *My goal is to make people feel at ease.* Calm confidence comes from being grounded and engaged, not from commanding attention.

Listening is your superpower. Use it to create warmth and connection. Make eye contact, nod, and show genuine interest in what others say. A simple smile, kind word, or thoughtful acknowledgment can go a long way. When people feel truly seen and heard, trust naturally follows.

Connection grows from being real. Don't chase perfection; share your ideas with sincerity and warmth. The leaders who leave a mark aren't flawless—they're genuine. That quiet confidence inspires trust and respect that lasts.

Your demeanor sets the emotional tone for everyone around you. When you bring calm, others feel safe. When you show gratitude, others feel valued. Stay composed under pressure, celebrate small wins, and express appreciation often. People may forget what you said, but they'll always remember how you made them feel.

Before any big moment, take a breath, stand tall, and smile. Visualize a positive outcome. Leadership isn't about performing—it's about connecting. When you show up with intention, calmness, and authenticity, you create a presence that inspires confidence, trust, and loyalty wherever you go.

3. Positive Attitude: Be the Energy You Want to See

Your attitude acts like the weather system swirling through your team. Will it be a bright, sunny day that lifts everyone's spirits or a gloomy, stormy environment that drags the mood down? I once worked at a location where employees, unfortunately, referred to a particular manager as *the dark cloud of doom*. Yep, not exactly the poster child for positivity.

A positive attitude doesn't mean you pretend problems don't exist. It's embracing resilience, radiating empathy, and tackling challenges with the mindset that every obstacle is simply a problem waiting for a clever solution. When you show up with optimism and a can-do spirit, it inspires the entire team. You're not just setting the tone—you're creating a cascading effect that encourages everyone to bring their best energy too. Let's explore ways to cultivate and display a positive attitude.

Resilience and Solutions

When challenges arise, don't treat them as roadblocks—see them as speed bumps that push you to think differently and get creative. If a project doesn't go as planned, resist the urge to assign blame or dwell on frustration. Stay calm, stay open, and lean in.

Approach setbacks with a solution-focused mindset. Say, "Okay, let's map this out. What happened, why did it happen, and what can we do to prevent it from happening again?" Invite collaboration, encourage reflection, and model resilience. By leading in this way, you create a safe space for learning, innovation, and trust, turning every misstep into a step forward.

I'll never forget my time in the Navy when our master chief set the tone during a particularly chaotic training drill. Equipment was failing, communication lines were tangled, and the team was fraying at the edges, with more than one of my teammates grumbling, "This is impossible." Instead of barking orders or assigning blame, he flashed a grin and said, "Impossible is nothing but a dare, and I love a good dare!" Suddenly, the team's energy shifted. We weren't just scrambling to fix problems—we were brainstorming, tossing out ideas, testing solutions, and laughing through the issues. His approach wasn't intended to deny the problem but to embrace the challenge and trust the team to rise to the occasion.

To this day, his simple but impactful words serve as a morning affirmation for me when I know I have a challenging day ahead of me.

Contrast that with the all-too-common scenes I've witnessed in other settings. A project hits a snag, and the room fills with a chorus of complaints: "It's never going to work!" "When is corporate going to step up and help us?" "I knew this was going to happen—we're doomed." Negativity spreads like poison ivy, draining morale and stifling progress. In those moments, I've found that a straightforward question can flip the script: "Okay, I agree, things are a bit off track, but what's one thing we can do right now to improve things? Just one." Make no mistake, this isn't ignoring the problem or pretending everything is fine. It's cutting through the drama and focusing on action. That question shifts the mood from helpless to determined, from stuck to solution oriented. Suddenly, people stop complaining and start contributing. Ideas flow, and momentum builds.

Don't just promote optimism, build a culture of resilience. Create an environment where challenges are met with curiosity, collaboration, and forward thinking, not fear or blame. Show your team that every problem has a solution worth uncovering. Model the mindset that progress comes from small, consistent actions. Break problems down. Focus on what can be done next, not what went wrong. Keep the team moving forward, one step at a time.

Make your expectations clear: Keep your door open, but also encourage ownership. If someone brings a problem, ask them to come with at least one possible solution. This empowers people to think critically, build confidence, and contribute to problem-solving.

Set the tone. Lead with action. Turn every challenge into a chance to grow.

Quick tip: Kick off your meetings with a little inspiration to set a positive tone! Try opening with a lighthearted, funny story, or tossing out a fun prompt, like "What's one thing you crushed this week?" It's a quick boost of positivity that lifts team morale and gets everyone engaged and smiling before diving into the agenda. I used to kick off the week with staff meetings every Monday morning. To shake off the Monday blues, I'd start by asking if anyone had a quirky or unexpected weekend story to share. And if the room went quiet? No problem—I always had a tale from my endlessly unpredictable life ready to go.

Empathy in Action

A good check-in isn't a robotic "How's your workload?" It's personal and natural, like chatting with a friend. If you notice someone's been quieter than usual or is overwhelmed with tasks, try something like, "Hey, you've been in beast mode lately. Is everything cool on your end?" It's casual but opens the door for them to share if they're stressed, overwhelmed, or need to vent about their dog chewing their favorite shoes. The key is to listen without jumping into Fix-It Felix mode. Sometimes, people want to be heard. And timing matters! Don't approach them mid-deadline. Instead, engage them during a coffee break or when things settle a bit. If they say, "I'm fine," but their demeanor speaks otherwise, gently reevaluate later. Subtle persistence shows you care.

Nothing says *I see you* like shouting out a job well done. Did someone crush a client pitch, debug a nightmarish piece of code, or survive a brutal week? Call it out: "Tyrone, you nailed that presentation today—honestly, the detail you provided helped our clients truly understand the why behind what we do!" It's not just praise—it's an invitation to share their moment of glory, which makes it memorable. Public recognition in a team meeting or casual one-on-one also helps, but keep it specific, no generic "Great job, team!" Ugh, there's nothing more disingenuous. Name the person, the win—and the impact it had. Empathy shines in the little things.

Kick-Start Your Day

Let's be honest: Not every morning comes with endless energy and a can-do attitude. Some days, we drag ourselves out of bed, navigating a mental haze instead of charging into the day. That's when a small, deliberate pick-me-up can shift everything, paving the way for an upbeat start.

In my home, I've created a small ritual to embrace positivity from the start. Tucked on the wall behind my coffee maker, the sacred spot I visit first each morning, hangs a modest canvas with an impactful reminder: "One small positive thought in the morning can change your whole day." These words serve as a gentle nudge, but their actual impact comes when I pause to let them sink in and actively reflect on something uplifting.

I often turn to gratitude to shake off the morning haze and cultivate a brighter mindset. It's a simple yet profound practice that shifts my perspective almost instantly. I might think about the people who light up my life, including my friends and family, or express appreciation for my career, the opportunities I've been given, or even something as lighthearted as still having a full head of hair. Mostly. These moments of gratitude, regardless of how big or small, serve as a mental reset, steering me toward a day filled with optimism and purpose.

Another tool I've embraced is the use of positive affirmations. I'll admit, when I first tried saying affirmations out loud, it felt strange, as if I were rehearsing for a role I wasn't sure I could play. But once I found affirmations that resonated with me, they became a natural part of my routine and genuinely worked.

These short statements help reframe my mindset, replacing doubt and negativity with confidence and possibility. Below, I've shared a collection of affirmations that have inspired me over time. Feel free to try them out, adapt them to suit your voice, or create entirely new ones that speak to your unique journey:

- I rise above negative thoughts and actions with ease and grace.

- I am blessed with countless talents and will make the most of them today.

- With a strong heart and a clear mind, there's nothing I can't achieve.

- Impossible is nothing but a dare, and I love a good dare.

- I am strong and resilient—others can count on me.

- My mind overflows with positivity, and my life is abundant.

- My body is vibrant, my mind is sharp, and my spirit is filled with joy.

- I hold the power to shape my life and create meaningful change.

By beginning my day with a moment of gratitude or a positive affirmation, I set the tone for a day filled with purpose, optimism, and endless possibilities. My intent is not to ignore life's challenges but to face them with a mindset that I'm ready to tackle anything. So, tomorrow morning, take a moment to discover your charge of positivity—it might transform your entire day!

4. The Benefits of Humor in Leadership

Humor is a transformative force in the workplace, igniting genuine emotions, fostering stronger team connections, making leaders more approachable, and building resilience in the face of pressure. When delivered effectively, it promotes camaraderie, reduces stress, and boosts morale, creating an environment where people excel. However, humor requires a delicate balance—context and delivery are crucial. Get it right, and you become a morale-boosting hero—misjudge the moment, and you risk undermining your credibility. Take the CEO, Brad, for example. He mastered using self-deprecating humor to charm the room and maintain a light, yet focused atmosphere.

Throughout my career, I've relied on humor as a key component of leadership, a practice rooted in my time as a Navy Seabee. Oh, you don't know what a Navy Seabee is? No problem, let me explain: A Navy Seabee is a member of the U.S. Navy's construction battalions (CBs), specialized units trained to build and maintain military infrastructure in diverse and often challenging environments. The term Seabee comes from the initials CB. Seabees are skilled in construction, engineering, and combat tactics, which enable them to construct bases, airfields, roads, bridges, and other facilities, often under combat conditions or in remote locations.

Initially, I expected the military to be a humor-free zone, characterized by rigid discipline and stern expressions. Instead, I discovered that humor served as a lifeline, boosting morale and enhancing performance under the most challenging conditions. My former commanding officer captured this in one of my annual evaluations: "Petty Officer Spence's sharp wit and keen sense of humor contribute to the success and morale of his subordinates and peers alike." This praise traces back to a pivotal moment during a deployment in Okinawa, where humor transformed a crisis into a manageable challenge.

Permission to Laugh

While stationed at Camp Shields, my unit was assigned the less-than-glamorous task of constructing a ball field for the Marines at Camp Hansen. We were knee-deep in excavation when we unearthed a nightmare: live World War II munitions buried beneath the site. Our construction project quickly morphed into a History Channel special. Work came to a halt and the team's hesitation was palpable, radiating like cheap cologne in a crowded elevator. As the tension threatened to unravel us, I decided to lean in to humor to steady the ship. Mixing self-enhancing humor with a touch of playful aggression, I quipped, "Guys, it's all good—we just need to stand perfectly still for, like, seventy-two hours until the EOD crew flies in from California. And (Bobby) Crawford, that should be a breeze for you since I haven't seen you move your ass in two years!" The team erupted in laughter, the suffocating tension dissolved, and as one quip led to another, suddenly our focus shifted and the mood lightened, regardless of the fact that we had just stumbled into a minefield.

This shift in mood was more than just comic relief—it paved the way for clear-headed collaboration. We huddled, brainstormed, and devised a plan to secure the site while we awaited the explosive ordnance disposal team. When my commanding officer arrived, he initially raised an eyebrow at the team's lighthearted demeanor. I responded, "Nothing for nothing, Skipper, but if there was ever a time for a laugh, it's now." He observed the team's renewed focus and problem-solving energy, nodded, and said, "Carry on." Bobby approached, asking, "What just happened?" I responded with: "Well, I believe we were just given permission to laugh." That moment crystallized the ability of humor to reframe disorder, unite people, and inspire action.

This wasn't a one-time occurrence—there were many! For example, during an assignment in Bremerton, Washington, our unit faced relentless rain that turned our construction site into a muddy swamp. Equipment was failing, deadlines were looming, and morale was sinking faster than our boots in the sludge. To lighten the mood, I initiated a running gag about our "new Seabee swim team," complete with exaggerated freestyle strokes while hauling gear through the mud. The absurdity had everyone chuckling, and soon we were exchanging quips about who'd win the "mud medley." That shared laughter didn't just uplift spirits—it created a sense of unity that carried us through the project, reinforcing our Seabee motto: Can Do.

These and many other experiences taught me that when wielded with care, humor is a vital leadership skill. It not only lightens the mood but also reframes challenges, strengthens bonds, and inspires innovative solutions. As Seabees, we embraced humor as a tool to navigate adversity. In any high-pressure environment, humor serves as an essential strategy that fosters resilience.

The Biology of Laughter

It's the dead of night. You're deep in sleep when—suddenly—a strange noise jolts you awake. Your heart slams in your chest, your breath quickens, and your senses snap to high alert. Instinct takes over. You're scanning the darkness, searching for the source. That rush of intensity? It's cortisol—your body's built-in alarm system—surging through you, readying you for whatever comes next.

In that instant, cortisol is a helpful partner, priming you for the fight or flight response—an ancient survival instinct that activates in the face of real or perceived threats. This physiological chain reaction, driven by the sympathetic nervous system, unleashes a flood of hormones and neural impulses to ramp up energy for either battling the peril head-on or fleeing from it.

Yet, for all its benefits, cortisol has a downside: Our bodies aren't great at distinguishing true dangers from everyday pressures. So when work stress hits, like a looming deadline or a tense meeting, your system treats it like a potential threat, pumping out hefty doses of the hormone. The trouble arises with chronic overloads, especially in environments characterized by intense ego clashes and backstabbing office dynamics, where tension escalates. Over time, this relentless cortisol flood can devastate health: It fogs memory, dials down immune defenses, and heightens the chance of depression, unwanted weight gain, and cardiovascular issues.

I've watched managers fume over "unjustified" sick days from staff, quick to dismiss them as excuses. But here's the reality: Toxic workplaces, fueled by fear-based leadership or ruthless rivalries, don't just grind down morale—they can actually make people ill.

Enter the Antidote

Laughter. Far from being mere feel-good fluff, laughter is supported by science. According to a 2023 Mayo Clinic article, "Stress Relief from Laughter: It's No Joke," laughter increases oxygen flow, triggers the release of endorphins, and calms the stress response. It relaxes muscles, reduces tension, and even serves as a natural pain reliever. Over time, it strengthens the immune system, helps fight depression, and boosts mood.[4] Employees struggle in workplaces dominated by fear, where threats of retribution for minor mistakes are common. However, a culture that embraces humor turns this around. Stress melts away, imaginations soar, and people genuinely want to come to work.

A Catalyst for Trust and Performance

Laughter is more than just a brief escape from stress—it's the glue that binds people together and fosters trust, especially when it comes to leading a team. At the heart of it, trust kicks in when folks feel safe enough to let their guard down, and humor does wonders by making leaders feel real and relatable, not like some far-off boss on a pedestal.

It works by adding that feeling of *Hey, we're all in this together.* Imagine a leader tossing out a self-deprecating joke or recounting a ridiculous office mishap—it instantly evens things out. Boom, the boss goes from intimidating overlord to *one of us*, with all the quirks and humanity that come with it. It's just like how you and your friends bond over those dumb inside jokes, creating that us-against-the-world feeling that makes everything click. In the office, it means your team starts feeling truly heard and appreciated, not just herded along.

And the best part is that humor creates a sense of belonging that strengthens trust. Studies back it up: Teams led by individuals who incorporate good-natured laughs tend to be more motivated and loyal, as it strengthens the feeling of being part of a team. Here's how.

Shared laughs pull everyone in: Drop a funny one-liner in a meeting, and suddenly a bunch of awkward strangers are cracking up together—it's like an instant "welcome to the club" invitation.

It softens the hierarchy: In those stiff, top-down setups, a bit of humor dials back the power trip, making it easier for people to speak up. Your team gets comfortable sharing worries with a leader who can laugh at themselves. And down the line, it toughens the whole group, laughing through the rough stuff turns trust into a shield against burnout and blowups.

Long before I entered the world of human resources, I had a deep passion for medicine. I studied all the core sciences— anatomy, biology, physiology, and more—and eventually became a paramedic. At one point, I even considered going to medical school, but life had other plans. That said, I still have a solid understanding of how the human body works.

Every now and then at work, someone will mention a symptom or minor injury, and I'll offer a bit of insight—always with the disclaimer: "But you should definitely see a professional." More often than not, they'll follow up with "Wait, how do you know all this?" That's when I get to deliver one of my favorite self-deprecating lines: "Well, I once thought about becoming a doctor . . . but then I realized that *really is* for smart people."

It always gets a laugh and makes me appear more approachable. Of course, I'd never pull out that line in a formal setting like a job interview—it could easily be misunderstood!

Humor in Action

Several years ago, I consulted for a transportation company that struggled with frequent vehicle accidents and property damage. The senior managers expressed a desire to establish a culture of accountability, so I was invited to attend several meetings as an observer and address these issues. The manager's approach? A tense meeting where he berated drivers, pointed his finger, and threatened their jobs. I couldn't help but mutter, "Holy crap," under my breath, loud enough to turn heads. My bad.

When the onslaught of intimidation and ridicule ceased, I scanned the room and observed nothing but demoralized and defeated employees. It broke my heart. Afterward, I met with the management team and was asked for feedback. I was candid: "Look, I understand you're all frustrated, I get it. But the fact is that fear doesn't breed accountability. Instead of ruling with intimidation and threats, try focusing on building meaningful and trusting relationships." After receiving some further advice and a bit of convincing, the company allowed me to initiate the next meeting.

I opened by asking, "How many of you have kids who drive?" Hands shot up, and I shared a lighthearted story regarding my teenage daughter, Samantha.

"It was a crisp Saturday morning, and my sixteen-year-old daughter, Sami, was behind the wheel of our family SUV, her

learner's permit still fresh in her purse. We were out for a practice drive, winding through the familiar streets of our suburban
neighborhood. I sat in the passenger seat, trying to balance my
role as both instructor and dad, offering pointers while resisting
the urge to grip the armrest too tightly.

"Sami was doing well—her turns were smooth, and her stops
were deliberate. However, as we circled back toward home, I
noticed her focus slipping. The radio blared a song she loved, and
her eyes darted to her phone, which was buzzing in the center
console. She wasn't texting, thank goodness, but the temptation
was there. I cleared my throat, aiming for a tone that was firm
but not overbearing.

"'You know, Sami,' I said, 'statistics show that over 50 percent of all auto accidents happen within a few miles of where we
live. People get too comfortable in their own neighborhoods.' She
didn't miss a beat. With a smirk and a quick glance my way, she
quipped, 'Well, maybe we should move!'"

The room erupted in laughter. That moment of connection—a
shared laugh, a relatable anecdote, a simple gesture—acted as a
catalyst, dismantling the invisible barriers that often stifle communication in workplace settings. This wasn't just a fleeting feel-
good instance—it fundamentally shifted the dynamic. Breaking
the ice created a psychological space where vulnerability and
authenticity could emerge, making everyone feel safer to share
ideas without fear of judgment.

I continued, presenting a series of driving scenarios and
actively soliciting their insights and recommendations. The
highly engaged response prompted me to swiftly capture their
ideas and suggestions on the nearest whiteboard.

The response from the leadership team was pivotal. Recognizing
the value of that moment, they didn't let it pass. They took notes

not only on the content of the discussion but also on the process and how the icebreaker resulted in openness. This led to a deliberate decision to integrate icebreakers into future meetings. The goal wasn't gimmicky fun—it was to create an environment where employees felt seen as individuals, not just workers.

Seeking employee input was the next critical step. Instead of top-down directives, the managers invited suggestions on safe driving practices. This empowered employees, giving them ownership over the solutions.

As a result, meetings evolved. Where they once felt like one-sided lectures, stiff, disengaging, and often ignored, they became dialogues. Employees started asking questions, challenging assumptions, and proposing ideas. The manager, now listening more than dictating, facilitated these exchanges, ensuring every voice was heard.

This dynamic shift established trust and open communication, an essential component of any effective team. Employees began to see the manager not as an enforcer but as a partner invested in their safety and success. Trust also fostered accountability—drivers were more likely to follow safe driving protocols because they had a hand in shaping them. Beyond metrics, morale improved, employees felt valued, and camaraderie grew.

By prioritizing connection, input, and trust, the manager transformed a routine safety discussion into a blueprint for lasting cultural change, proving that small, intentional acts can yield transformative results.

The Ability of a Humorous Culture

Before we jump into this section, let's take a moment to talk about culture, because you have seen that word throughout this book. How to build it, what makes it strong, and why it matters.

But first, ask yourself: What does *culture* really mean? At its core, culture is simply the common values and beliefs shared by a group of people. When you create a culture that truly reflects those values and hire leaders who genuinely believe in them, you set your organization and people up to thrive.

If trust is one of those core values (and I hope it is), it becomes the foundation for happiness, equality, respect, opportunity, loyalty, and excellence that benefits everyone. That's not just a good culture; that's a great culture.

A thriving workplace culture operates like a well-oiled machine, running smoothly and efficiently when all parts work in harmony. Friction, caused by mistrust, poor communication, or misaligned priorities, generates heat, leading to stress, disengagement, and breakdowns in collaboration. Trust serves as the oil, lubricating interactions and fostering mutual respect. Humor, meanwhile, acts as the refinery, transforming raw interactions into moments of connection and levity, while simultaneously building trust by humanizing leaders and revealing their vulnerability. When leaders skillfully leverage humor, they break down barriers, becoming more approachable and relatable, which encourages open dialogue in return. Employees, in turn, feel valued and empowered rather than micromanaged or overlooked. The result is a culture of happier teams and fearless ideas. A culture that not only survives but prospers, driving innovation and loyalty.

However, not all humor is created equal, and its impact depends on how it's wielded. Leaders must recognize that humor comes in four distinct styles, each with its own unique flavor, strengths, and potential pitfalls. By understanding and mastering these styles, leaders can tailor their approach to suit their team's dynamics, maximize engagement, and cultivate a workplace where innovation and collaboration thrive. Let's examine these four styles to ensure you get it right!

Affiliative Humor: The Heart-Warmer

The sun is setting, and a cool, gentle breeze blows through the air as a crackling campfire burns on the beach. Its warm glow draws everyone in, igniting instant connection and a sense of togetherness. That's affiliative humor, the kind of light, feel-good wit that wraps everyone in a blanket of laughter without compromising the feelings of others. It's the ultimate crowd-pleaser.

Take this example from my days as the humor resources leader, excuse me, *human* resources leader, at a manufacturing plant. The maintenance supervisor, Chuck Spagnola, faced a tense morning. The night shift had botched a critical weld on some newly installed structural beams, delaying production and souring the day shift's mood. Grumbles echoed through the break room as workers sipped coffee, their frustration palpable.

Chuck, known for his steady hand and sharp wit, stepped onto the shop floor with a plan to not just fix the welds but lift his team's spirits. He gathered his crew of welders, machinists, and assemblers around the faulty beams. "All right, folks," he said, his eyes twinkling, "looks like our beams got a case of the Monday blues on a Wednesday. Who's ready to play doctor?"

The team chuckled, the tension easing. Chuck grabbed a welding helmet, flipped it on with a dramatic flourish, and mimicked a surgeon's voice. "Scalpel—I mean, torch—please!" The workers laughed as he pretended to operate on the beam, narrating with mock seriousness. "We're going in, people."

His humor was gentle, inclusive, pulling everyone in to the moment. He handed the torch to Manuel, a shy welder, and said, "You're up, Doc. Show this beam some love." The crew cheered Manuel on, and soon, the group was trading lighthearted jabs about their own welding surgeries. The mood shifted—the team worked together, fixing the beams with precision and camaraderie.

By lunch, it was all back on track, and the shop floor buzzed with energy. Chuck's affiliative humor hadn't just defused the frustration—it had *welded* his team closer.

This style is my go-to because it welcomes everyone to the party. No sharp jabs, no divisive quips, just pure, relatable fun that brings people closer. In the workplace, affiliative humor is a manager's secret weapon. It serves as the perfect morale booster, keeping spirits high and teams connected. Being kind and inclusive ensures that no one is left out or belittled. From a clever one-liner to a shared laugh over life's little quirks, this heartwarming humor leaves everyone grinning, connected, and ready to take on the day.

Self-Enhancing Humor: The Optimist's Choice

Self-enhancing humor feels like wearing rose-colored glasses that make every life's hiccup appear as though it's a scene from a sitcom where you're the star. It's the go-to strategy for resilient individuals, spotting the absurdity in the mayhem while keeping your head held high and your mood light.

This humor style is your trusty sidekick when life throws a wrench your way. For instance, when my HR team and I were excited about a big Vegas trade show, our Uber driver dropped us off at the wrong hotel. Bummer, right? We were a bit annoyed, with meetings to prepare for and all. But instead of sulking, one of my colleagues decided to quote the hilarious Ron White. "Hey," he said, "If life gives you lemons, you should make lemonade and try to find somebody whose life has given them vodka and have a party!" He motioned to the bar. "Now there's a guy who has vodka!" So we grabbed some drinks, shared some laughs, and turned the mix-up into a mini party. Oh, and we totally (probably) made it to the show on time!

I once used self-enhancing humor to increase my chance of winning $500!

During the COVID lockdown, like many others, I found myself scrambling to set up a home office. As this became a shared experience, someone on LinkedIn came up with a clever idea: a contest called My Work-From-Home Crib, a playful spoof of MTV's Cribs, the show that showcased the extravagant homes of celebrities.

The premise was simple: Submit a video tour of your new home workspace, your work-from-home crib. The prize? A cool $500. With no strict rules or judging criteria, many of the entries I saw felt a bit uninspired. So, I seized the opportunity.

Enter my Aquatic Cubicle. Picture me in a hot tub (clothed), fully equipped to take on a day's workload. I went all in, highlighting the importance of a comfortable, stress-free work environment, complete with all the necessary office equipment, including a built-in bathroom to boost productivity. It was my way of taking a tough situation and using humor to lighten the mood.

Curious to see it? You can check out the video on my YouTube channel: https://www.youtube.com/c/BartSpence/videos

Oh, and yes, I did win the contest, though I'm still waiting on that check . . .

To summarize, you're not ignoring the problem. You're chuckling with it, not at it, and that's what keeps you moving forward. Why is this a big deal? Self-enhancing humor acts like mental armor. It builds resilience, lifts your spirits, and makes you the kind of person others are naturally drawn to. It promotes open communication and nurtures genuine honesty.

Self-Deprecating Humor: The Humble Chuckle

Self-deprecating humor is like intentionally walking into a closed door for a laugh. I could entertain you with stories of my expert-level faceplants, but we can save those for another time. Instead, let me share a tale of biblical proportions.

My kids grew up Catholic—school, church, the whole experience—and I'm proud of how it shaped them. I'm not Catholic myself, but I enjoyed joining family events, including Sunday Mass. Mostly. Communion was always tricky. You know, everyone receives the wafer and wine, but if you're not Catholic, you either stay seated (which felt rude to me) or walk up with your arms crossed in a big X. I don't mind saying that I felt pretty darn awkward, but I wanted to support the family, so off I went, crossed arms and all.

One Sunday, I saw my favorite monsignor, a familiar face at the chalice, who always had a great sense of humor. I saw my chance. Instead of crossing my arms, I made an L with my fingers and held it to my forehead. The monsignor grinned and said, "Bart, you're no loser!" I shot back, "I know, Monsignor, I'm Lutheran!" He barely held in his laugh, and I felt a sense of belonging at that moment. Just to be clear, I meant no disrespect—my heart was in the right place!

Self-deprecating humor involves poking fun at your own quirks, failures, or downright embarrassing moments. Consider it a way to transform your personal blooper into a stand-up routine.

I recall a coworker, Dave, who was notorious for his inability to complete tasks on time. He once quipped, "It's not that I'm lazy. I'm energy efficient."

This kind of humor serves as a social Swiss Army knife. It can make you seem approachable, defuse tension, or even earn you points for humility. When Dave laughs at his own time-management trainwreck, he's not just owning it—he's inviting everyone else to nod along and admit, *Yeah, I've got my own messes, too.* Think of it as a group therapy session disguised as a one-liner that invites open and honest communication.

But here's the catch: Like eating an entire family-size bag of Doritos by yourself, there's a fine line between fun and *Oh no, why did I do that?* Lean too hard into self-deprecating humor, and you might start sounding like you're fishing for compliments or, worse, like you've got a PhD in self-sabotage. Imagine Dave cracking the same "I'm energy efficient" joke every week. By week three, the team's not laughing—they're side-eyeing each other, wondering if Dave's actually okay or if HR needs to stage an intervention. If you overdo it, you risk painting yourself as the office's lovable-but-incompetent mascot. Nobody wants to be the guy who's only good for a laugh.

So, how do you wield this comedic skill without crashing and burning? Keep it authentic, not performative. Laugh at your quirks, not your entire existence. Add it lightly, like hot sauce—just enough to enhance the flavor, not so much that everyone's in tears. And pair it with confidence. Dave's joke lands because he's smirking, not sulking. He's saying, *I'm a mess sometimes, but I'm still here, and I'm owning it.* That's the sweet spot, where self-deprecating humor isn't just a chuckle, but a mic-drop moment that shouts, *I'm human, I'm hilarious, and I've got this . . . mostly.*

Aggressive Humor: The Razor-Sharp Zinger

Visualize a verbal fencing match where every jab is infused with sharp sarcasm, precise ridicule, or a piercing remark designed to leave a lasting impact. Aggressive humor is the comedic equivalent of a lightning bolt: electrifying when it strikes just right but potentially searing if it falls flat. Consider the legendary Don Rickles, the sultan of sting, whose rapid-fire insults could bring a room to hysterics while teetering on the brink of discomfort. His style was a masterclass in wielding humor like a scalpel, slicing through egos with surgical precision.

This brand of humor thrives on audacity. The bold, unapologetic quip catches everyone off guard, producing laughter through sheer shock value. But beware, it's a risky game. Nail the punch perfectly, and you're the life of the party—misjudge your audience, and you risk alienating friends, colleagues, or even strangers. The line between hilarious and hurtful is razor-thin, and aggressive humor dances on that edge with reckless abandon.

In settings like the workplace, this style is particularly risky. A sarcastic hook or a mocking jab might feel like a playful nudge to you, but for someone else, it could land like a sucker punch. Workplace dynamics are already a minefield of egos and sensitivities, and aggressive humor can easily escalate tensions or breed resentment. Unless you're a comedic genius with Rickles-level charm and impeccable timing, it's wise to sheath this particular weapon in the office. Save the sharp-tongued zingers for a roast among close friends who know your heart is in the right place, or better yet, channel that wit into something less likely to cause harm.

Now, if you're saying to yourself, *But I'm not funny and I'm terrible at telling jokes, nor do I possess lightning-fast wit*, don't sweat it. Below, I'll discuss the basic structure of humor, followed by some practical tips to help you develop your ability to use humor as a leadership skill

The Anatomy of Humor

Humor isn't an elusive talent exclusive to comedians or those naturally equipped with wit. It's a craft that can be dissected, examined, and mastered, just like any other mode of expression.

The basic structure of most humor breaks down into two key elements: setup and punchline.

Setup: This is the foundation where you establish a normal, expected scenario. It draws the audience in by painting a familiar picture, often using everyday observations, self-deprecation, or shared experiences. The goal is to create a predictable mental frame. For example, in a leadership meeting: "We've all been in those endless strategy sessions where the coffee runs out before the ideas do . . ."

Punchline: This is the release, the twist that manipulates the expectation. It should be concise, timed well, and land with just enough surprise to gain a chuckle or smile, without overexplaining. Continuing the example: ". . . which is why today, I'm proposing we start with the donuts and work our way back to the budget." The humor arises from the absurdity—flipping the serious (strategy) with the absurd (prioritizing snacks).

Other Common Structures

Rule of three: List two expected items, then hit with a third that's unexpected. Example: "Leadership requires vision, execution, and enough caffeine to power a small city."

Callback: Refer back to an earlier joke or point later in the conversation for reinforcement, creating a sense of continuity and cleverness.

Exaggeration: Amplify a truth to absurd levels for effect. Example: "Our team's deadline is so tight, even light couldn't escape it."

In leadership, the structure should align with your goals; use it to develop inclusivity, not exclusion. Avoid punch-down humor (targeting the vulnerable) and aim for punch-up or self-directed wit to build trust.

Steps to Learn How to Use Humor—Yes, Even If You're Not Naturally Funny

Humor as a leadership skill requires practice, observation, and achieving small wins, not relying on natural talent. It's like building a muscle: Start light, be consistent, and refine based on feedback. Here's a step-by-step guide to develop it practically.

Observe and Analyze Humor Around You

Spend time studying what makes others laugh. Watch stand-up specials or TED Talks with humorous elements. One of my all-time favorites is the TED Talk "Do schools kill creativity?" performed by Sir Ken Robinson. I recommend watching it and then breaking it down. What was the setup? Where was the twist?

It's absolutely brilliant!

In daily life, note funny moments in meetings, emails, or conversations. Keep a humor journal where you jot down three to five examples per day, analyzing their structure. This builds your intuition without pressure.

Tip: Focus on relatable, observational humor rather than complex puns at first—it's easier to replicate.

Begin Modestly Using Secure, Low-Risk Exercises

Begin in noncritical settings, like casual chats with trusted colleagues or friends. Try simple self-deprecating lines, like "I'm the kind of leader who plans everything . . . except my coffee breaks."

Use written formats first if speaking feels daunting—add light humor to emails or reports. Example: "Here's the attached quarterly report. Good news: We're still in the black . . . and the coffee fund is fully stocked!"

Set a goal: Incorporate one humorous element per day or meeting. Track what lands and what doesn't—no judgment, just data.

Master Timing and Delivery

Humor is 50 percent content, 50 percent delivery. Practice in front of a mirror or record yourself. Pause after the setup for anticipation, then deliver the punchline with a straight face or slight smile.

Read the room; humor works best when it's relevant and timely. In leadership, tie it to the topic. If discussing a failed project, say, "Well, that idea bombed harder than my attempt at karaoke last year."

If a joke flops, have a recovery, such as: "Tough crowd! Moving on . . ." This shows resilience and keeps things light.

Seek Feedback and Refine

After using humor, ask for honest input. "Did that land okay, or should I stick to pie charts?" Use it to refine your style. You may consider joining groups like Toastmasters, that teach spontaneity without the risk.

Measure impact: In leadership, note if humor improves engagement or morale. Adjust accordingly—humor should enhance, not distract.

Avoid Common Pitfalls and Build Confidence

Steer clear of sensitive topics (such as politics, religion, or personal traits). Focus on inclusive, positive humor.

If you're introverted, lean on prepared lines rather than improv. Over time, confidence grows. Remember, even "unfunny" people, such as introverted leaders (Warren Buffett and Bill Gates), can use dry humor effectively.

Be patient: It might take weeks or months, but consistency pays off. Celebrate small successes, like a colleague's smile.

By following these steps, you'll turn humor into a deliberate tool, making you a more approachable, effective leader. It's not about being hilarious—it's about connecting authentically. If you practice, you'll surprise yourself—and others.

Overcoming the Barriers

To make leadership a powerful, approachable, and effective force, it's essential to intentionally recognize and tackle hidden barriers that hinder growth and innovation. By applying practical solutions to these challenges, leaders can unleash their full potential and drive impactful change within their teams and organizations. Below are some key barriers to effective leadership transformation, along with comprehensive strategies to overcome them.

Barrier: Inconsistent behavior

When a leader's behavior swings from friendly one day to distant or reactive the next, it creates an uneasy atmosphere. The team starts walking on eggshells, unsure of what version of their leader they'll get. This kind of unpredictability makes it hard to focus, communicate openly, or feel safe taking risks.

And when favoritism enters the mix, where only a few people get recognition or opportunities while others are overlooked, it can quickly damage morale. Resentment builds, trust erodes, and soon the team's overall performance takes a hit.

Strategy: Build emotional awareness

Becoming a leader your team feels comfortable with starts with emotional awareness, understanding how your behavior and energy impact the people around you. The goal isn't to be perfect, but to be consistent, fair, and human. Here's how.

1. Build self-awareness

- **Do regular emotional check-ins:** Before you head into meetings or conversations, pause and ask yourself: *How am I feeling right now? Is that going to affect how I show up?* Tools like journaling or quick mindfulness breaks can help you spot patterns and stay grounded.

- **Get honest feedback:** Ask trusted coworkers or mentors how you come across. Are there times when you seem unpredictable or distant? You can also use anonymous surveys to get candid feedback without putting anyone on the spot.

- **Pause before reacting:** Stressful moments happen. Instead of reacting in the moment, take a breath, count to ten, or step away briefly. Small pauses can prevent big blowups.

2. Be emotionally consistent

- Set a steady tone: You don't need to fake positivity, but try to bring a consistent, steady demeanor to your team. If you're having a rough day, it's okay to say something like "I'm a bit off today, but I'm focused and here for you." That honesty builds trust.

- **Be clear and predictable:** When people know what to expect from you, how you make decisions, what's acceptable, and what isn't, it reduces anxiety and confusion.

- **Lead with calm during chaos:** When things go sideways, show your team how to stay calm and solution-focused. They'll follow your lead.

3. Eliminate favoritism

- Be fair with opportunities: Take a step back and look at who's getting the prime assignments, recognition, or face time. Is it balanced? If not, fix it. Make fairness the standard.

- **Recognize everyone:** Shout out wins from different team members, not just the same few. A quick mention in a meeting or message goes a long way toward making everyone feel seen.

4. Build real connections

- Show you care: Take the time to learn about your team—their goals, challenges, and strengths. Small gestures like checking in or asking how a project is going can build trust fast.

- **Create a safe space:** Encourage people to speak up, share ideas, or raise concerns, without fear of a negative reaction. Handle feedback (even tough stuff) with curiosity, not defensiveness.

When you lead with awareness, consistency, and fairness, everything changes. People feel valued, empowered, and more willing to contribute. Over time, trust grows, and with it, productivity, innovation, and real team connection.

Barrier: Time constraints

We get it, everyone's busy. Between meetings, deadlines, and overflowing inboxes, it's tough to find time for a genuine human connection at work. But when those moments disappear, so does the sense of team. People start to feel more like task machines than valued contributors, which leads to burnout and disengagement.

Strategy: Make time for real connection

You don't need hour-long meetings or big events to build team culture. Even small, intentional moments can make a big difference.

Use micro-moments: Try brief, agenda-free check-ins—just five minutes to ask how someone's doing or bounce around ideas. These can happen at the start of meetings or during breaks and don't need to feel forced.

Block out connection time: Set aside a weekly *open hour* for informal chats, brainstorming, or team catch-ups with no pressure to be productive. Treat it like any other important meeting, it's a nonnegotiable time to reconnect.

Offer flexible options: Create optional drop-in times—whether it's a recurring Zoom room or a casual in-person lounge slot—so people can join when it works for them. Rotate the times so everyone has a chance to participate, no matter their schedule.

The bottom line is, you don't need to choose between productivity and connection. With a bit of intention, you can have both, and when you do, your team will be stronger, happier, and more effective.

Call to Action

Developing the third principle of approachable leadership involves creating the perfect balance for a dynamic, invigorating, and inspiring presence! To help master this leadership style, I've provided a few actionable steps to help you achieve this.

Enhance positive communication skills: Choose a topic you're passionate about (a hobby, a recent project, or a positive idea). Record yourself giving a one-minute explanation of the topic. Focus on:

- Speaking at a moderate pace with clear enunciation
- Using an enthusiastic tone to convey excitement (vary pitch, emphasize key points)

Play back the recording and evaluate:

- Was your speech clear and easy to understand? Did your tone convey enthusiasm and positivity?
- Repeat the exercise, incorporating feedback from friends or family to improve clarity and enthusiasm.

Tip: Smile while speaking to enhance the warmth of your tone naturally.

Cultivate an approachable appearance: Build awareness of your current appearance and demeanor. Find a quiet space, stand or sit in front of a mirror, or use a front-facing camera on your phone to observe yourself and assess your baseline.

- **Smile:** Smile naturally and observe how it feels. Is it forced or genuine? Pay attention to how your eyes and mouth appear when you smile genuinely. Slight crinkling around the eyes is a sign of a genuine smile.

- **Posture:** Stand or sit naturally. Observe your shoulders. Are they tense or relaxed? Are your arms crossed or open? Open is preferred, as closed arms signal unapproachability. Observe your body position. Is it slumped or upright? Note what feels comfortable or tense.

- **Clothing:** Reflect on what you're wearing today. Does it feel authentic to your personality and the image you want to project? Does it make you feel confident and approachable?

- **Journal your observations:** Write down your initial impressions of your smile, posture, and clothing. Note areas where you feel you could improve to appear more approachable.

Establish a can-do attitude: Begin tomorrow by choosing a positive affirmation. You can select one from this chapter that speaks to you or craft your own. Repeat it at home and during your commute to set a confident tone for the day. It might feel unusual initially, but with time, you'll notice its uplifting effect.

"Laughter is more than just a brief escape from stress—it's the glue that binds people together and fosters trust, especially when it comes to leading a team."

NOTES

NOTES

CHAPTER FOUR: THE 4TH PRINCIPLE

RESPECT

Respect in the workplace starts with a simple truth: People matter.

It's not just about being polite, following protocol, or checking the boxes of professional courtesy. True respect goes deeper—it means genuinely recognizing and appreciating the unique strengths, perspectives, and contributions that each person brings to the team. Whether someone is leading a department, navigating their first role, or building their path somewhere in between, they deserve to feel seen, heard, and valued. Respect shows up in how we listen, how we communicate, how we give credit, and how we make space for others to grow.

When people feel respected, they're more likely to speak up, share ideas, and collaborate openly. Respect creates a space where individuals feel safe to be themselves—and where diverse backgrounds, experiences, and perspectives aren't just accepted, but genuinely valued.

Respect doesn't mean constant agreement. It means listening without judgment, being open to feedback, and treating others with kindness—even when things get challenging. A respectful workplace builds stronger relationships, boosts morale, and drives better results. It lays the groundwork for a culture where people can do their best work and feel good doing it.

This isn't just theory—research backs it up. A 2025 study published in the journal *Psychological Reports* explored what respect really means at work and developed a way to measure it. The authors, Swati Dir and Tanusree Dutta, looked at things like feeling accepted, having autonomy, and being free from discrimination. Their findings showed that when employees feel genuinely respected, they're more likely to connect with the company and see themselves as part of it—which can lead to stronger performance across the board.5

However, respect can't just live in a policy or on a poster. It has to be woven into the daily fabric of your organization. The fourth principle offers a clear path for making respect a lived, lasting part of your culture.

Respect as a Foundation

Your vision and mission statements should act as your North Star, radiating a clear and unmistakable message: *Respect is who we are and how we operate.* These statements aren't just decorative—they're a rallying cry. Your core values, meanwhile, should function as a detailed playbook, guiding everyone's behavior, from the C-suite to the newest intern, in every interaction, decision, and moment of truth.

Take a hard look at your organization and ask: Do our mission and vision statements make respect an absolute, nonnegotiable priority? Are our core values more than words? Do they live and breathe as a practical guide for how we treat one another, day in and day out? If you're nodding confidently, that's a great start.

But if there's even a hint of hesitation, it's time to roll up your sleeves and get to work. Your mission, vision, and values should mirror an organization where respect is the default, not the exception. But before we proceed, I feel it's prudent to define the difference between mission, vision, and value statements.

Mission statement: A mission statement defines the organization's current purpose, what it does, who it serves, and how it operates right now. It's practical and action-oriented, guiding daily decisions and operations. It answers the question: What are we doing today?

Vision statement: A vision statement outlines the long-term aspiration, where the organization wants to be in the future. It's inspirational and forward-looking, motivating stakeholders toward a big-picture goal. It answers the question: What do we want to achieve ultimately?

Values statement: A values statement articulates the core principles that guide behavior, culture, and decision-making. It describes the beliefs and standards that shape how the organization and its people act. It answers the question: What do we stand for and how will we accomplish it?

I've partnered with numerous teams across diverse industries, including tech startups, healthcare providers, manufacturing firms, and nonprofits, to dig deep and define what respect truly means to them. In discovery sessions, we don't just skim the surface. We ask tough, soul-searching questions: Is respect about actively listening without interrupting, even when tensions run high? Is it valuing every perspective from the corner office to the cubicle? Does it mean celebrating differences, not just tolerating them but embracing them as a source of strength?

These conversations transform abstract ideals into mission statements and values that resonate deeply, reflecting the organization's unique identity and aspirations. But make no mistake: As mentioned, this exercise is a discovery—it's not inventing what an organization believes will be popular. This is what you truly believe—otherwise, the lack of authenticity will become evident as your attempts to implement and sustain your values lack impact. This exercise should sound familiar, as it mirrors the exercise described in Chapter 1—identifying your core values to achieve moral courage. However, this applies to the entire organization.

Here is an example of an excerpt from a vision (what and why) and values (what and how) statement:

Vision excerpt: At XYZ Corporation, we envision a world where every individual who engages with our organization is not only deeply respected but also enveloped in a profound sense of belonging, igniting their potential to thrive and contribute without reservation.

Values excerpt: Respect—we champion respect as our guiding principle, nurturing it with unwavering dedication to empathetic leadership, transparent and heartfelt dialogue, and the relentless cultivation of a truly equitable culture where every voice is heard and every spirit is uplifted.

But let's look at the hard truth: Words alone are not enough, no matter how eloquently crafted. A mission or vision statement hanging on a wall or a set of values printed in an employee handbook won't change anything unless they're brought to life. Respect must leap off the page and into the daily rhythm of your organization.

This is where the real work begins. You need a roadmap and a clear, actionable plan to embed respect into every corner of your workplace. This means defining behaviors that demonstrate respect, such as giving constructive feedback with empathy or ensuring every voice is heard in meetings. It involves crafting policies and reinforcing fairness and inclusion, from equitable hiring practices to transparent conflict resolution processes. Last, it requires taking deliberate actions like training leaders to model respect and recognizing employees who embody it.

Something that makes respect so special is that it's not a one-size-fits-all deal. What feels respectful to one person might not resonate with someone else, due to their unique values, cultural background, or personal quirks. Disrespect is just as personal. There's no universal rulebook for respect, hence why we need to tune in, be thoughtful, and adapt to what makes each person feel valued.

A Lunchtime Lesson on Building Connections

One afternoon, an employee came to me with a concern. Her manager, trying to be a good team leader, kept organizing team lunches. Sounds fun, right? But there's a catch: The restaurant was a vegetarian's nightmare. As someone who didn't eat meat, Melinda was left nibbling on a sad side salad while her coworkers chowed down on burgers.

Now, this wasn't simply a lackluster lunch menu. The real kicker was that her manager seemed to know everything about the rest of the team: Dave's obsession with soccer, Lisa's love for jazz, even Gilbert's weird ketchup-on-everything habit. But her vegetarianism was totally off his radar. To her, this wasn't just about food—it was a sign he didn't care enough to notice what made her unique.

At first, I thought, *Is this a big deal?* But then it clicked. Respect extends far beyond epic gestures, such as throwing a party or giving a corner office. It's the little things, like knowing your team's passions, quirks, or, yep, even their food preferences. Great leaders are like detectives, picking up on the details that make people feel seen, whether it's their favorite hobby, cultural traditions, or whether they'd rather hug a cow than eat one. Moo.

A leader who had taken the time to know their team would've caught this. A quick chat weeks earlier—"Hey, any dietary preferences for lunch?"—could've ensured a thoughtful veggie option. That small gesture screams, *I see you, and you matter.* It's the little moves that make a massive impact.

When we were children, our parents often taught us to treat others as *we* would like to be treated. However, as leaders, treating others based on how *they* wish to be treated is far more effective. This requires understanding their preferences and perspectives.

Getting to know employees personally builds respect by building trust, empathy, and stronger interpersonal connections. When leaders take time to understand employees' backgrounds, interests, and motivations, it signals genuine care, making team members feel valued and appreciated. This creates a positive work environment where mutual respect thrives. Specifically, it:

- **Builds trust:** Personal connections demonstrate to employees that they're valued as individuals, not just for their roles, creating openness and loyalty.

- **Enhances empathy:** Understanding personal

circumstances enables leaders to respond compassionately, thereby strengthening relationships.

- **Improves communication:** Understanding employees' communication styles creates more transparent and respectful interactions.

- **Lifts team spirit:** When leaders take the time to recognize people's hard work, whether it's a shout-out in a meeting or a quick thank-you message, it really makes a difference. It shows employees that what they do matters, and that kind of appreciation goes a long way. When people feel seen and valued, they're more motivated, more engaged, and more likely to bring their best to the team. It also strengthens the connection between leaders and their teams, building trust and mutual respect.

- **Brings people together:** Getting to know each other on a personal level helps teams feel more connected. When trust and real relationships are in place, it's easier to face challenges as a group. People are more open, more willing to listen, and less likely to butt heads over disagreements. Instead of turning into arguments, tough conversations are handled with empathy and understanding. That sense of respect for different opinions leads to better ideas, smoother teamwork, and an all-around more productive and positive environment.

Let's say you're passing by a colleague at work and you ask,

"How was your weekend?" Then, instead of settling for a bland "Good," you dig deeper. "Really? Tell me more. What made it great? Try anything new? Catch a new show?" Before you know it, you discover they're quietly training for a 10K, adopting shelter dogs, or perfecting artisanal bread. These aren't just fun facts—they're the foundation of trust, connection, and a team that feels like family.

Another story illustrates this point. While I was serving as the human resources leader at a manufacturing plant, we held monthly happy hours off-site to create an environment where everyone could get to know each other. During one of our events, a manager noticed that one of her quieter team members, Alex, always remained on the sidelines. Instead of assuming Alex was just antisocial, she became curious. During a casual one-on-one, she asked, "What's your hobby outside of work? Got any passions we don't know about?"

It turned out that Alex was an avid charcuterie enthusiast who spent weekends perfecting artful boards with cured meats, cheeses, and creative garnishes. The manager didn't stop there— she suggested a team charcuterie night, allowing Alex to take the lead in organizing it. Alex brought a stunning spread, teaching the team about flavor pairings and board design. Not only did Alex shine, but the team also bonded over slicing salami and sampling cheeses, uncovering shared interests they'd never have discovered otherwise. That's the benefit of knowing your people—it turns coworkers into collaborators and workplaces into spaces where everyone feels valued.

To get things rolling in your organization, try setting aside ten minutes weekly for a no-work, get-to-know-you chat with a teammate. Just talk about their life. These conversations reveal what matters to them, helping you lead with empathy and establish solid connections. You'll know when to offer flexibility for a family event, celebrate a milestone, or check in during tough times. But keep in mind that this isn't a one-time effort. Building these bonds is ongoing. Regularly check in. Notice when someone's off and ask, "You okay?" It's also important to acknowledge their successes, big or small. Over time, these moments create a culture where people don't just show up and work for a paycheck—they show up because they feel they belong.

Crafting Respect Through Mindful Tone

Words have real power, but the way you say them—the tone—often hits even harder. It can turn a simple sentence into a bridge that builds a real connection or a catalyst that starts a fight. I've seen it play out many times: An employee calls out a boss's disrespectful approach, or a coworker feels stung after a quick chat, not because of what was said but how it landed. A snappy, offhand tone can turn an innocent request into bad blood that lingers, while something warm and considered builds trust and teamwork.

Getting the tone right is crucial for earning respect and strengthening relationships in every conversation. This sets the stage for how your message comes across, paving the way for what's next. A rushed or sarcastic approach can twist helpful feedback into a personal dig, but a steady, empathetic delivery transforms tough conversations into chances for real bonding. Before you jump in, just pause and consider: *How might this tone land with them?* Make sure it lines up with what you really want to achieve.

That quick breather is extremely valuable, especially when things heat up, so you don't fire off an email or a snap reply you wish you could take back (guilty as charged). Even a couple of seconds lets you check your own headspace: *Is stress, frustration, or distraction sneaking in?* Those can slip into your tone without you noticing. Breathe, zero in on your aim—maybe to motivate, clarify, or inspire—and adjust your delivery to fit, so your words carry the respect and intent you mean. Sure, everyone tunes in differently depending on their style, so being flexible makes tone a tool you can tweak for the person and the moment.

A direct, no-frills approach might motivate a go-getter colleague, but it may push away someone who needs that team feeling. Pay attention to their subtle signals, such as their body language or past experiences, to understand what works for them. For example, steering a frazzled team with a calm, backing-you-up tone can boost their confidence and spirits, while a sharp, nitpicky tone wears them down. By watching and shifting gears, you craft conversations that feel custom and considerate.

And tone is more than just what you say—it's in how you listen too, reflecting the care you give others. When you reply, work in real empathy with a nod, solid eye contact, and something like "Got it, that makes sense, let's keep going." It shows you value their view and delivers that same respect right back, turning thoughtful tone into a good connection.

Mastering tone, like any other professional skill, takes consistent, intentional practice. Start small. In your next meeting or casual conversation, focus on speaking a bit more slowly and softly. Pay attention to how you can convey warmth, confidence, or precision depending on the context.

Consider partnering with a trusted mentor or colleague who can provide honest feedback and help you fine-tune your communication style. Below is an example of how to construct these types of exercises.

Mentoring Exercise

Schedule a thirty-minute weekly session with your mentor to strengthen your communication and executive presence. Choose a week or two to focus on tone and delivery in professional conversations. Use the time to role-play real scenarios, gather feedback, and set one or two actionable goals to practice before your next meeting.

Step 1: Observation and Feedback

Your mentor asks you to describe a recent meeting where you felt your tone might not have landed well. You replay what you said and how you said it. Your mentor listens, then shares. Example: "You made your point clearly, but your tone sounded a bit rushed and firm—almost like you were shutting down discussion. Try slowing down and softening your voice to invite more dialogue."

Step 2: Role-Play and Experimentation

Next, you and your mentor role-play a scenario—perhaps a project update to your team. You practice delivering the same message twice:

- Once using your *usual tone*

- Once with a *calmer, more deliberate tone*, adding pauses and a gentle inflection

Your mentor notes the difference and gives feedback. Example: "The second time, your tone sounded more approachable. People would feel safer speaking up."

Step 3: Real-World Practice

Your mentor encourages you to apply this in your next team check-in and suggests a small, specific goal. Example: "Focus on slowing down your speech and using a lighter tone when responding to questions." You make a mental note to pause before answering and check: *Does my tone reflect what I truly mean?*

Step 4: Reflection and Adjustment

At your next meeting, you share how it went. Example: "I noticed I spoke more calmly, and the discussion flowed better. But when I got excited about a new idea, I sped up again." Your mentor responds: "That's progress. Awareness is the key. Next time, catch yourself in that excitement and balance enthusiasm with clarity."

With time, you'll develop an intuitive ability to adjust your tone to fit the moment. If you misstep, and it happens to everyone, own it. A simple "I didn't mean to sound that way, let me rephrase" can rebuild connection and respect. Tone isn't just a minor detail—it's a key factor in how others interpret your words and intentions. By staying aware of your tone, pausing to ensure it aligns with your message, and tailoring it to your audience, you can transform routine interactions into moments that build trust and respect. Before you speak, ask yourself: *Does my tone reflect what I truly mean?* A touch of mindfulness can create conversations that make everyone feel heard and valued.

Celebrate What Makes Us Different

Imagine a world where everyone looked, thought, and acted the same—a flat, colorless version of life. It'd be boring, predictable, and honestly, pretty uninspiring. What makes life (and work) interesting are our differences—our cultures, experiences, perspectives, and even our quirks. These are what bring depth and energy to our workplaces, communities, and relationships.

Embracing what makes each of us unique isn't just about being kind or fair—it's the key to sparking creativity and building real, meaningful connections.

When we genuinely value what sets people apart, we create spaces where new ideas flourish, teamwork strengthens, and respect becomes the foundation for genuine progress. Different perspectives challenge our thinking, open our minds, and lead to solutions we wouldn't find in a room filled with identical voices. This kind of environment helps everyone feel like they belong—that their voice matters and their contributions count.

Here are a few practical tips for mixing it up and embracing the awesomeness of our differences.

Invite Creative Solutions

Got a tricky problem that's stumped your team? Don't keep it locked in the same old meeting room! Instead, pull up some extra chairs and invite a diverse mix of voices from various teams to join the conversation. I've shared insights before on tackling root cause analysis, and let me tell you, this approach is a game changer. Bringing in someone with an original perspective who isn't entrenched in the usual routine can shed new light on the issue, uncover innovative ideas, and break through those stubborn roadblocks.

This goes far beyond just solving problems—encouraging cross-team collaboration encourages bold ideas, builds mutual respect across departments, and fosters a stronger sense of unity throughout the organization, leading to impactful solutions, happier teams, and a workplace that hums with energy and possibility!

Throw Epic Events

Ditch the dull, predictable office parties with bland food and forced chit-chat. It's time to elevate your event into a vibrant, one-of-a-kind celebration that reflects your team's unique spirit! Assemble a dynamic event-planning crew, pulling in colleagues from diverse backgrounds, departments, and perspectives to inspire creative ideas.

Dream big and collaborate. Design a menu featuring delicious dishes that honor the diverse cultures within your team. Encourage colleagues to contribute their own recipes or traditions, and consider partnering with local restaurants or cultural organizations to ensure authenticity and depth.

Keep the momentum going with thoughtful, engaging activities—invite a local artist to create a mural that reflects your team's values, set up a DIY station for personalized keepsakes, or plan entertainment that aligns with your team's interests. The goal is to create a welcoming, memorable experience that brings people together and leaves a lasting impression. It's a celebration of your team's unique spirit—genuine, meaningful, and uplifting.

Turn Language Barriers into Bridges

In today's diverse workplaces, language differences don't have to be hurdles—they can become opportunities for connection. Imagine hosting fun, low-pressure phrase exchanges where team members teach each other everyday words or greetings from their own lives. One person might share how to say *thank you* in Mandarin, another might introduce a favorite Italian expression their grandmother always used. At the same time, someone else might bring a playful slang phrase that promotes laughter.

These sessions go far beyond vocabulary—they create moments of joy, mutual respect, and curiosity. As people swap phrases, share the stories behind them, and highlight the richness of their cultural roots, you'll see your workplace transform into a vibrant hub where every voice is heard, valued, and celebrated.

Shake Up Leadership

You're sitting in a meeting, eating day-old donuts, and someone drops the classic line, "If only I were in charge, things would be different!" Cue the eye rolls, right? But hold up, what if we let them take the wheel? Not forever, mind you, but just long enough to stir the pot, create some magic, and maybe, just maybe, uncover a few leadership rockstars hiding in plain sight. Welcome to the wonderful world of *Shake Up Leadership*, where passion meets opportunity, and the status quo gets a courteous shove out the door!

This isn't flipping the org chart upside down or handing the CEO's chair to the intern (though, wouldn't that be a story?). It's giving nontraditional leaders, those fiery, idea-bursting folks who don't usually wear the boss hat, a chance to step up temporarily and show what they've got. Think of it like a leadership audition.

Now, if you're feeling a little reserved about this exercise, don't! There are few things more restricting to an organization than working in silos. They're like invisible walls that keep departments from communicating and thriving. By empowering passionate people from every part of the organization to step into leadership roles, you're dismantling barriers. Plus, it's a boost to confidence. Picture the quiet coder or the positive receptionist suddenly realizing they can rally a team, pitch an idea, or solve a problem no one else noticed. That's the kind of energy that transforms workplaces.

And let's be real: This isn't just chaos. It's controlled chaos, the fun kind! You're not handing over the company keys and saying, "Good luck!" Instead, set clear goals, give them a short-term project or a single meeting to lead, and watch them shine. Maybe it's the warehouse guy running a brainstorming session or the marketing assistant pitching a new campaign. You're promoting new voices, uncovering innovative perspectives, and reminding everyone that leadership isn't tied to a title—it's fueled by passion, guts, and a dash of originality.

The best part? It's contagious. When people see their coworkers stepping up, they start thinking, *Hey, I could do that too!* Suddenly, you've got a workplace buzzing with confidence, collaboration, and ideas that wouldn't have emerged in the usual top-down setup. Plus, it's a low-risk way to identify future leaders. That quirky IT specialist who excelled in their temporary leadership role might be your next project manager.

Here's how to make it happen: Start small. Choose a low-risk project or meeting, invite volunteers, or nominate enthusiastic individuals who don't usually receive the spotlight. Provide them with a clear mission, some coaching if necessary, and allow them to take the lead. Celebrate their successes, learn from their failures, and maintain the momentum.

Hone Your Skills to Earn Lasting Respect

Building respect—whether at work or in your personal life—is about more than just being nice or creating a positive demeanor. While things like treating people well and building solid relationships matter a lot, they're not always enough on their own. One of the biggest pieces of the puzzle is being good at what you do.

If people don't see you as skilled or capable, it's tough to earn their respect—no matter how friendly or collaborative you are. Competence builds trust. It shows others you're dependable, confident, and someone they can count on. But don't stress—you don't have to be perfect. Developing your skills is a process, not an event. There's always room to grow, and here's how you can focus on leveling up.

Sharpen your skills: Getting really good at something takes time—and even the pros keep learning. Make learning a regular part of your routine, whether that's through classes, online courses, mentorship, or just getting curious and teaching yourself. Push into areas you're less familiar with. For example:

- In tech? Learn a new tool or language.

- In a creative role? Try out different styles or study the greats in your field.

Practice with purpose: It's not just about putting in hours—it's about how you spend them. What's the saying? "It's not practice makes perfect—it's perfect practice." Pick specific skills you want to improve, set goals, and ask for feedback. If you're a public speaker, record yourself and look for ways to improve. If you're a writer, write daily and seek honest feedback from trusted peers. The more intentional you are, the faster you'll grow.

Let your work speak for itself: You don't need to brag. Just keep showing up, delivering solid results, and solving problems. That's what earns real respect. Whether it's hitting deadlines or offering brilliant insights during a meeting, your consistency will speak volumes. And remember—stay humble. Quiet confidence tends to make a stronger impression than loud self-promotion.

Keep up with change: Things move fast. What worked a few years ago might be outdated today (just ask Blockbuster). Staying on top of your game means keeping up with trends and changes in your field. Some examples:

- A developer might learn a new language or framework.

- An HR pro might stay updated on evolving laws or hiring practices.

Staying current shows that you're engaged and forward-thinking.

Keep growing: Being great at what you do means consistently delivering and always looking to improve. It's not about being perfect—it's about effort, consistency, and a willingness to learn. When you combine skill with kindness, integrity, and collaboration, respect will follow.

So stick with it. Every step you take to improve moves you closer to becoming someone others trust, admire, and look up to. Keep learning, keep growing—and let your work speak for itself.

Gauge Your Roadmap with Feedback

A roadmap is not a static document—it's a dynamic framework that grows with your organization. Regular evaluations are essential to determine what's effective and what needs adjustment. Are employees feeling appreciated? Are leaders modeling the desired behavior? Do discrepancies exist between your stated values and actual practices? Refine your strategy by collecting feedback through surveys, focus groups, or individual discussions to ensure respect remains a core pillar of your culture. I recommend anonymous surveys, like those on SurveyMonkey, to create a safe space for honest input.

Avoid vague questions such as "Do you feel respected at work?" or "Does your manager treat you respectfully?" These lack the specificity needed to identify what's working or where improvements are required. Consider this: If a leader is found to lack respect toward their team, simply instructing them to be more respectful is as ineffective as telling a short person they need to be taller. These questions do not explain why respect is present or absent. I recommend using statements with a scoring scale, such as *Always*, *Usually*, *Occasionally*, or *Never*. I excluded a neutral option, as everyone experiences respect or its absence to some degree.

Here are a few suggested statements you can utilize for your respect survey:

1. My manager takes the time to learn about me personally.

2. I feel that my supervisor values my contributions to the team.

3. I feel included and respected regardless of my personal characteristics.

4. My manager provides constructive feedback in a respectful and supportive manner.

5. The workplace culture promotes respect for differences in background, gender, race, or beliefs.

6. I believe respect is a core value upheld throughout the organization.

You can also add a question or two that require direct responses:

7. Have you personally experienced any form of disrespect in the workplace in the past year? Yes / No

8. If yes, please describe:

_____

_____

Overcoming the Barriers

Creating a workplace where respect is the foundation of a culture is a worthy goal, but it's not without its challenges. From unconscious biases to communication breakdowns, barriers to respect can undermine teamwork, productivity, and morale. However, these obstacles can be addressed with intentional, practical, and effective strategies. Below, we explore common barriers to building a respectful workplace and provide actionable steps to overcome them, ensuring an environment where every employee feels valued and empowered.

Barrier: Workplace conflict

Workplace conflict is an inevitable part of any professional environment where diverse individuals come together to collaborate. With different backgrounds, perspectives, and personalities in the mix, occasional friction is bound to happen. Whether it's a disagreement over project priorities, clashing work styles, or a simple miscommunication, conflict often emerges not from bad intentions but from differing expectations or unclear communication.

Strategy: Address conflict promptly

Disagreements are a natural part of collaboration, and when managed effectively, they can spark fresh ideas, fuel innovation, and strengthen team dynamics, all without the unnecessary drama. The key is not avoiding conflict but knowing how to navigate it with clarity, respect, and intention.

Here's how to keep conversations constructive and the momentum moving in the right direction:

- **Jump in quickly:** Don't let issues fester into a soap opera.

- **Stay on topic:** Concentrate on the issue, not the individual.

- **Stay open:** Innovative ideas could be game changers.

- **Experience the mood:** A nod to emotions does wonders.

- **Listen closely:** Tune in, refrain from judging, and truly hear them out.

Barrier: Lack of recognition

Nothing stings quite like pouring your heart and soul into your work, only to have your efforts go unnoticed. The absence of recognition in the workplace can be a silent morale-killer, eroding motivation and leaving employees feeling undervalued and disrespected. When contributions are consistently overlooked, it has a cumulative effect: Enthusiasm dwindles, productivity stagnates, and team spirit suffers. Over time, this lack of acknowledgment can lead to disengagement, causing employees to question their purpose within the organization.

Strategy: Recognize and reward contributions

Recognizing and rewarding contributions, whether monumental or incremental, can ignite motivation, boost morale, and sustain positive momentum. By celebrating all victories, big or small, organizations can cultivate an environment where employees feel valued and inspired to excel. Here are a few steps you can take to make recognition a consistent part of your workplace.

- **Shout it out:** Utilize team huddles or company chats to celebrate outstanding efforts—everyone appreciates a moment in the spotlight.

- **Pass the mic:** Allow coworkers to give kudos to one another.

- **Connect it to values:** Emphasize how excellent work embodies the company's core principles.

- **Be prompt:** Acknowledge achievements while they are still fresh, not six months later.

- **Make it personal:** Some people love public praise, while others prefer a quiet "Nice job." Understand your audience!

Barrier: Lack of awareness

One significant obstacle to respectful communication and behavior is a lack of awareness. Often, individuals may not fully recognize that their words, actions, or behaviors could be perceived as disrespectful, offensive, or inappropriate by others. This oversight can stem from cultural differences, personal biases, or simply a lack of exposure to diverse perspectives. Without proper guidance, these unintentional missteps can lead to misunderstandings or harm relationships in personal, professional, or social contexts.

Strategy: Respect workshops

Objective: Provide hands-on training to define and demonstrate respectful behavior in various workplace scenarios. You may want to contact your HR department with this concept to gain their input and support.

Format: Interactive workshops led by experienced facilitators, incorporating role-playing, group discussions, and case studies. If you do not have a qualified person in-house, you can recruit a third party for this exercise.

Topic examples:

- **Respectful communication:** Techniques for active listening, constructive feedback, and managing difficult conversations with empathy and clarity.

- **Professional behavior:** Understanding boundaries, maintaining professionalism in high-pressure situations, and promoting inclusivity.

- **Workplace etiquette:** Best practices for email communication, meeting conduct, collaboration in shared spaces, and virtual interactions.

Frequency: I would recommend annual workshops for all employees (including management), with additional sessions for new hires during onboarding.

Call to Action

Building a culture of respect requires ongoing, genuine dedication and deliberate efforts to make sure every individual feels equally valued, listened to, and honored. Here are a few immediate steps you can take to advance this objective.

Connect with your team: Start by choosing just three individuals: direct reports, peers, or external partners. Jot down their names and aim to learn all you can regarding their aspirations, concerns, hobbies, and interests. Avoid making it feel like an interrogation—keep the conversation light and natural. Share some details about yourself to build trust and encourage openness. Record what you discover about each person and commit it to memory. Now, choose three more and repeat!

Build trust through open communication: Within the next week, schedule a dedicated meeting with your team members to create a safe space for them to share their thoughts, concerns, and ideas. Encourage honest dialogue by setting clear expectations that all perspectives are valued and will be heard without judgment.

During conversations, practice active listening by giving your full attention to the speaker, avoiding interruptions, and summarizing their key points to ensure understanding. Publicly acknowledge contributions to reinforce a sense of appreciation and trust.

Follow up on the meeting by addressing concerns raised and sharing progress on discussed action items. For example, send a brief recap email that summarizes key takeaways and outlines the next steps.

Practice your tone: Partner with a reliable colleague to rehearse giving tough feedback. Guide them on key elements to observe, like your vocal tone and nonverbal cues. Let them evaluate your overall approach. Their immediate response will offer valuable early insights. Accept the input openly and tweak your style accordingly.

*"Respect doesn't mean constant agreement.
It means listening without judgment, being
open to feedback, and treating others with
kindness—even when things get challenging."*

NOTES

NOTES

CHAPTER FIVE: THE 5TH PRINCIPLE

DELIVERING FEEDBACK

Performance review season is here, and the office is buzzing with anticipation! It's time to sit down with your leader, celebrate your wins, and chart a path for growth. But sometimes, the event takes a nosedive: *Underperforming? I thought I was crushing it!* That gut-punch moment often comes from feedback being a once-a-year guest star rather than a daily occurrence.

When leaders skip regular feedback opportunities, they miss the chance to inspire their teams. Feedback isn't a mundane task—it's a vital component of building trust. It catalyzes performance and overall success! By incorporating open and honest conversations into their daily routine, leaders can unlock potential, align with goals, and cultivate a workplace that's practically buzzing with awesomeness. Ongoing feedback removes surprises during review season and nurtures a culture where everyone feels valued, energized, and ready to shine brightly.

And the data backs this up. Research by Gallup and Workhuman found that employees who strongly agree they receive valuable feedback from the people they work with are *five times more likely to be engaged in their jobs*.6 This kind of feedback—specific, timely, and meaningful—does more than help people improve their performance; it makes them feel seen, supported, and connected to their team and organization. The study also showed that frequent, high-quality feedback is linked to lower levels of burnout and a reduced likelihood of employees wanting to leave their jobs. In other words, when employees feel that their contributions are noticed and their development is supported through ongoing feedback, they're more likely to trust their workplace, stay committed, and perform at their best.

Let's be clear: The absence of regular, constructive, and positive feedback is the number one reason leaders fail to motivate, inspire, and build trust. Yep, it's that important.

The Silent Leader

In the sunny hills of Napa, California, Morgan Vineyards prospered under CEO Sydney Morgan. Her knack for bold wines transformed a small plot into a bustling winery with fifty passionate employees. However, Sydney had a quirk: She rarely shared feedback.

Her team poured their hearts into crafting wines and pitching ideas, but Sydney's response was often a nod, a quick "Tastes good," or silence. It left everyone guessing.

Consider Crystal, a talented winemaker. She spent weeks perfecting an organic Cabernet Sauvignon, hoping to impress Sydney. After presenting it, Sydney sipped, said, "Bottle it," and left. Crystal felt deflated. Was it bold enough? Too oaky? Unsure, she felt her confidence dwindle.

Then there was Michael, the marketing whiz. He pitched a vibrant campaign for a new rosé, but Sydney just jotted notes and moved on to harvest talk. Michael launched it, unsure if it hit the mark and feeling adrift.

Sydney's silence cast a shadow. The team stopped taking risks—new blends and creative labels seemed too risky without guidance. The winery's inspiration faded, and whispers grew: "Does she even notice?" Turnover crept up as talent fled to vineyards where their work was celebrated.

One sunny afternoon, Crystal and Michael gathered the team among the vines to discuss the issue. They invited Sydney, hoping for a change. Crystal spoke up: "Sydney, we love working here, but we need feedback to grow. We're guessing what you want." Michael added, "It's tough to innovate when we're in the dark."

Sydney felt surprised. She believed her silence signaled trust, not neglect. "I didn't want to hover," she said. However, hearing her team's struggles resonated with her. She vowed to step up.

The change wasn't instant. Sydney started small, praising a vintner's Merlot twist and offering feedback on a label design. It felt clunky at first, but the team lit up. Crystal beamed when Sydney raved about her Cabernet's depth. Michael's next campaign surged with Sydney's input.

Morgan Vineyards didn't transform overnight. Rebuilding trust was necessary, but Sydney's efforts reignited the winery's spirit. She learned that leadership involves much more than just vision—it's guiding the people who bring it to life. Silence, she realized, doesn't promote—it stifles potential.

The fifth principle provides an examination of the various aspects of delivering feedback that promotes communication and strengthens relationships.

Share Clear, Encouraging Feedback

Vague, half-hearted comments like Sydney's "Tastes good" or "Bottle it" are like serving flat, room-temperature champagne at a party: Nobody's excited, and the atmosphere falls flat! Instead, provide specific and enthusiastic feedback that packs a punch and keeps the energy escalating. Celebrate the standout moments with brilliance. Rave about Crystal's Cabernet with its leaders—its velvety depth and rich, lingering finish that steals the show. Then, incorporate constructive pointers to fuel improvement and maintain that creative momentum. It's like injecting your team with a double shot of confidence and inspiration, igniting their passion and driving them to elevate their craft to the next level!

Open Communication

Start an exchange of ideas by creating a relaxed environment where everyone feels heard and connected. Consider Sydney's case: Her quiet, reserved demeanor unintentionally came off as disengaging, making her team hesitant to share their wildest thoughts. To address this, cultivate a laid-back, no-judgment zone where everyone is eager to speak up. Perhaps you're hosting a casual team hangout with an easygoing atmosphere that breaks down barriers, encouraging debates and ideas. You can achieve the same results with casual brainstorming sessions, open-door discussions, or casual check-ins that lead to honest conversations.

Listen to genuinely understand where others are coming from, rather than simply tossing in your two cents. Celebrate everyone's contributions, ask thoughtful questions, and embrace diverse perspectives. This shows that every voice matters.

Show Appreciation for Effort

When Sydney overlooked recognizing Crystal and Michael's hard work, it dampened the team's spirit and momentum. Acknowledging everyone's contributions, even through small gestures, can boost workplace energy and maintain a positive atmosphere. A heartfelt thank you note or recognition of standout efforts, like Crystal's clever twist on a Merlot blend or Michael's eye-catching label design, can promote enthusiasm and confidence, inspiring others to bring their A game. Celebrating these wins strengthens team connections and creates a warm, supportive environment where everyone feels motivated to channel their ideas and passion into shared goals.

Trust but Verify

Borrow a page from President Reagan's playbook: Trust but verify. Sydney's hands-off leadership style might have seemed empowering at first. However, without clear direction, her team wandered like wine tourists lost in Napa's endless vineyards, feeling somewhat dazed and confused. Trust is the heart of any stellar team, but simply tossing tasks over the fence and crossing your fingers can lead to disorder.

Outstanding leadership requires balancing trust with the right amount of guidance. Let's say you're the captain of a ship navigating uncharted seas. You trust your crew to handle their responsibilities, but you don't allow the ship to drift aimlessly. You set a clear course, check the compass, and adjust the sails when necessary. Sydney nailed this with her game-changing tips on Michael's campaign. Her gentle nudges provided just enough structure to keep things on track without micromanaging, steering everyone toward the big win.

To lead effectively, embrace coaching moments that inspire and clarify. Connect with your team, not to micromanage but to ensure they have the tools, focus, and energy needed to excel. Think of yourself as their GPS, providing real-time suggestions, adjusting when they veer off course, and celebrating their successes with mini celebrations. By combining trust with proactive support, you inspire your team to face challenges while keeping the finish line clearly in sight. So, trust your crew, but always confirm they are on the right path.

Adapt and Learn from Feedback

Effective leadership involves openness to feedback and a commitment to continually adjusting your approach to meet your team's evolving needs. To lead effectively, stay receptive to input, adaptable to change, and committed to tailoring your style to your team's unique requirements.

Consider Sydney's story as a fun example. She was cruising along as a leader, feeling quite confident, until her team shared some honest feedback during a heart-to-heart session. Instead of brushing it off, Sydney did what great leaders do: She listened, reflected, and took action. The results spoke for themselves: a team filled with renewed energy and cohesion.

1. Structure Your Feedback

Many leaders struggle with providing feedback for a number of potential reasons: lack of confidence, fear of retaliation, fear of alienation, and more. This is where having a structured model can be helpful. A clear and thoughtful approach to giving verbal and written feedback ensures consistency and thoroughness. Here's a four-step process I have found highly effective throughout my career. I call it the CARE method: Condition-Action-Result-Expectations.

In the example below, the CARE method is used as a means of feedback to help improve a situation.

Tip: Don't allow your feedback to sound like an attack. Maintain positivity and respect, ensuring you preserve the recipient's self-esteem and encourage a positive outcome.

Step 1: Communicate the Conditions

The first step is to ground your feedback in a vivid, specific context. Picture yourself as the director of a blockbuster movie: You need to establish the *when*, *where*, and *what* to pull your audience (the feedback recipient) right into the scene. Avoid vague references like "that one time last week." Pinpoint the exact moment and place of the action to jog their memory and eliminate confusion. A clear understanding of the conditions sets the stage for relevant and fair feedback, ensuring that everyone's on the same page.

Example: "During yesterday's team strategy meeting, we had an in-depth discussion about the Q3 project timeline and resource allocation."

By anchoring feedback in a specific moment, you help the recipient clearly recall the event, making the conversation feel like a constructive dialogue rather than an ambush.

Step 2: Analyze the Action

Now, focus on what actually happened, the raw, observable action. This isn't the time for guesswork, assumptions, or diving into anyone's intentions. Channel your inner detective and report only what you saw or heard, as if you're presenting evidence in court. Staying factual builds trust and prevents defensiveness, as you're not accusing them of *being* a certain way—you're merely describing what they did. This clarity ensures your feedback is credible and actionable, paving the way for a productive conversation.

Example: "During the discussion, there were a couple of moments when Clair and Tom were sharing their ideas for streamlining the project workflow, and you jumped in before they had finished. The conversation then shifted to your proposal, but their points weren't fully acknowledged."

Notice how this focuses on observable actions, such as interrupting and redirecting, without speculating about motives or labeling the action as rude. This approach keeps the feedback neutral and focused, making it easier for the recipient to engage without feeling attacked.

Step 3: Reveal the Result

You seal the deal by connecting the action to its results. Explain why the result matters, whether it resulted in a positive change or caused a hiccup. This is your chance to illustrate how their actions affected the team, the project, or their reputation. You inspire accountability and motivate action by linking the details to tangible outcomes. Be specific in relation to the results, whether it's a boost in morale or a roadblock to progress, to ensure the feedback resonates both emotionally and intellectually.

Example: "As a result of those interruptions, Clair and Tom stepped back from the conversation, and some valuable ideas may not have made it to the table. This impacted the team's collaborative energy and may have slowed our momentum in finding the most creative solutions."

Step 4: Establish Expectations

Establishing expectations is crucial in any process, whether it's project management, team collaboration, or personal goal setting. This step clearly outlines the desired outcomes, roles, responsibilities, and standards to ensure alignment and accountability.

Example: "Moving forward, it might be helpful for you and your team to focus on practicing active listening and being fully present when others are speaking. Taking a moment to acknowledge their ideas and thank them for sharing before adding your own can go a long way. It helps strengthen working relationships and contributes to a more positive, collaborative environment for everyone."

This example clearly outlines the specific details of the expectations, providing a comprehensive understanding of what is required. Additionally, it effectively highlights the many benefits of meeting these expectations, offering a well-rounded perspective on the advantages and outcomes.

2. Seizing Every Feedback Moment

Great leaders understand that feedback isn't merely another task to complete. It serves as the foundation for building trust, enhancing performance, and unlocking potential. But let's be honest: Time constraints, busy schedules, and logistic challenges can seem like massive roadblocks. I've witnessed it, heard about it, and experienced it firsthand. Nevertheless, the reality is that without feedback, there's no progress.

Let's explore some opportunities to make feedback a transformative experience!

Structured One-on-One Sessions

Schedule time for personal one-on-one chats to celebrate successes, address challenges, and align on goals—they're your ticket to building trust and demonstrating your commitment to your team's growth. Come prepared like a pro with notes, metrics, and updates, and advise your teammate to bring their topics to discuss. Start with a friendly "How's it going?" to set a positive tone, then listen attentively, leaving your ego at the door. Someone once told me, "Your ego is not your amigo." Love it! Reflect with something like, "It sounds like X is weighing on you," to show your engagement. Encourage deeper insights with open-ended questions like, "What's got you energized?" or "What's holding you back?"

Maintain balance by celebrating their wins and providing constructive feedback with clear examples and actionable tips. Stay flexible and accommodating, allowing for any unexpected topics to keep the conversation authentic. Finally, turn the tables and ask how these chats are working—it shows you're open to growth as well. Want additional tips on gathering feedback? Dive in to Chapter 6!

Real-Time Feedback

Don't wait for a formal meeting to speak up—jump in now. When you see something great, say it. When something's off, steer it back on course. Real-time feedback keeps the team sharp, aligned, and moving fast.

Celebrate wins as they happen. A quick "Nice work!" or "That was awesome—love it!" does more than make someone's day—it reinforces what's working and keeps the momentum alive. See a moment for improvement? Address it right then with clarity and care. A timely "Let's try this angle instead" can save hours down the line.

Leaders play a crucial role here. The best ones don't just give feedback in the moment, they do it with intention. They listen fully, let someone finish their thought, and then respond with insight that moves the conversation forward. This approach builds trust, encourages open dialogue, and models how to give feedback that's both immediate and respectful.

This isn't just about correction—it's about creating a culture of growth. When feedback flows freely, without delay, without ego, it becomes part of the rhythm. Stay flexible, stay vocal, and keep things moving. When everyone's tuned in and responsive, collaboration thrives and progress becomes the norm.

Team Debrief

Gather the team for an engaging post-project or quarterly retrospective focused on connecting, reflecting, and enhancing the team's awesomeness! I'm a total sucker for these sessions—they not only bring everyone together for growth, but they also offer the perfect excuse to bring in pizza—pepperoni and pineapple, please!

These debriefs are your team's golden opportunity to unite and celebrate those epic collective wins that make you want to high-five everyone in sight. However, they're not just for celebrations—they also offer a chance to shine a constructive spotlight on where we can adjust, improve, and grow even stronger. Think of it as a team huddle that's part strategy and part soul, where honest conversations flow, insights are shared, and everyone leaves feeling a little wiser and a lot more connected.

Forget typical feedback sessions filled with boring charts and forced smiles. This is an opportunity to engage in genuine conversations, share a few laughs, and create a culture where learning and fun are seamlessly intertwined. So grab your favorite pizza, gather the team, and make this debrief a highlight of the season!

Tech-Powered Feedback

I'm a massive believer in face-to-face interactions. Seriously, I thrive on the energy of being in the same room, bouncing ideas around, cracking jokes, and just soaking up the energy. Nothing compares. I still cringe when I think back to those post–COVID lockdown days, when I found myself stuck in a string of online speaking gigs. Brutal. Talking into a camera, staring at a sea of muted squares, with zero crowd energy? It felt like trying to high-five a brick wall. Hard pass.

But the reality is we're fully immersed in the hybrid work era. The lines between in-person and remote work have blurred, and the way we connect is evolving fast. Technology isn't just playing a supporting role anymore—it's center stage. These tools aren't flashy extras; they're the glue holding modern collaboration together.

Whether your team is in the office, working from their Aquatic Cubicle, or logging in from another time zone, today's platforms keep everything moving. Performance tools help track progress, pulse surveys deliver real-time insights into team morale, and chat platforms keep conversations flowing and teams aligned.

So don't let physical distance become a barrier to meaningful connection. Lean into the tech—use it to amplify human interaction, not replace it. This isn't about giving up the in-person moments we value; it's about making sure feedback and real conversation happen consistently, no matter where work (or life) takes us.

Mentorship and Coaching

Transform feedback into an energizing catalyst for growth by integrating it into dynamic mentorship or coaching programs. Mentoring and coaching are both valuable tools for supporting professional and personal development, but they serve different purposes and operate in distinct ways.

Mentoring is about long-term personal and career growth. It's usually a more relaxed, informal relationship where the mentor, someone with experience in the same field, shares advice, stories, and lessons they've learned along the way. The focus isn't on quick fixes but on guiding the mentee as they grow and figure things out for themselves. Feedback often comes up naturally during chats or check-ins and is usually based on the mentor's own experiences. For example, a mentor might say, "Here's what worked for me . . . " or ask, "Have you thought about trying this?"

Coaching, on the other hand, is more structured and focused on short-term goals or improving specific skills. A coach doesn't need to be an expert in your field, they're more like a guide who helps you stay on track using things like goal setting, action plans, and regular feedback. Coaching sessions are usually scheduled and focused, with feedback that's direct and tied to clear results. A coach might say something like "Let's talk about how that meeting went. What did you notice?" or give targeted suggestions for improvement.

Both mentoring and coaching offer great feedback opportunities, but coaching is generally more formal and goal driven, while mentoring is more about big-picture growth and support.

Overcoming the Barriers

Giving feedback is a key part of great leadership. It helps

people grow, boosts performance, and tightens team dynamics. However, delivering feedback, both positive and negative, is not always straightforward. Various roadblocks can present themselves, and leaders must determine how to navigate them. By identifying these hurdles and employing some effective strategies to overcome them, you can make feedback more helpful and ensure it actually lands well. Below, we will explore some common barriers to providing feedback, along with practical strategies to address each of them.

Barrier: Fear of negative reactions

The fear of negative reactions is a common barrier in communication, collaboration, and decision-making, particularly when delivering feedback or addressing sensitive topics. All too often, this fear stems from anticipation that the recipient might respond with defensiveness, anger, hurt feelings, or even retaliation, which can hinder open dialogue and progress.

Strategy: Build a culture of open communication

1. Make feedback routine: Establish feedback as a natural part of team dynamics. This helps to take the edge off and make it feel less intimidating. Encourage both positive and constructive feedback as a standard practice during team meetings and one-on-one check-ins. One example is developing a routine where team members share one piece of positive feedback and one suggestion for improvement at the end of each project milestone. This consistent practice helps feedback become a habit, creating a culture where it's expected and valued rather than feared or avoided.

2. Model receptiveness: Leaders play a significant role in shaping a feedback-friendly environment by demonstrating openness to receiving input. Leaders should regularly seek feedback from their teams, whether through anonymous surveys, open-door policies, or direct questions during meetings, and respond to it thoughtfully. For instance, a leader might share how they've acted on past feedback to show its impact. "Hey everyone, based on the feedback I recently received about the break room, we will now be offering a variety of teas and coffee at no charge. Thanks to everyone for your feedback." Another version: "Thank you to everyone who provided feedback regarding my use of my cell phone during meetings. I was not aware of the disruption it was creating, but rest assured that moving forward, my phone will rest quietly in my office during our meetings."

By visibly embracing feedback without defensiveness and expressing gratitude for input, leaders set a powerful example, reinforcing that feedback is a collaborative tool for growth, not a personal critique.

Barrier: Lack of confidence

Lack of confidence represents a significant barrier for leaders when delivering feedback, particularly in situations that involve sensitive, complex, or emotionally charged issues. This hesitation is typically the result of an array of underlying factors that contribute to a leader's reluctance or discomfort in engaging in meaningful feedback conversations. I have many times had leaders ask for my advice, or even for me to lead the discussion, because they are concerned about how the person will react, uncertain how to frame the conversation, or worried that the person may no longer like or respect them.

This lack of confidence can lead to avoidance of feedback discussions altogether, resulting in missed opportunities for growth, miscommunication, or unresolved performance issues within teams.

Strategy: Structure and practice feedback

Embracing structured feedback involves adopting a systematic, empathetic, and clear approach to ensure feedback is constructive, actionable, and well received. Below is an expanded strategy for leaders to enhance their ability to deliver feedback, particularly in challenging or sensitive situations.

1. Use a structured framework: The CARE model mentioned earlier in this chapter is an excellent framework for guiding a leader's feedback. With continued use, it will help to instill confidence with all varieties of feedback. If feedback results in assigning goals, using the SMART Goal framework described in Chapter 2 is an excellent addition to the CARE framework.

2. Practice empathy and active listening: Sensitive issues often carry emotional weight, so leaders must approach these conversations with empathy.

- **Acknowledge emotions:** Validate the recipient's feelings by saying, "I understand this might be difficult to hear," or "I appreciate your efforts in this area."

- **Use inclusive language:** Frame feedback as a collaborative effort. Example: "Let's work together to find a solution."

- **Listen actively:** Allow the recipient to respond, ask questions, or share their perspective. Paraphrase their input to show understanding. Example: "It sounds like you felt overwhelmed during that project, is that right?"

- **Avoid defensiveness:** If the recipient pushes back, stay calm and focus on problem-solving rather than escalating tension.

Call to Action

A leader providing feedback is invaluable because it encourages growth, enhances performance, and strengthens team dynamics. Here are some actions you can take right now to practice your feedback skills.

Apply the CARE model: The next time you're at work, find someone to provide one-on-one feedback to. You don't need to wait for a mistake—find someone doing something well and offer positive feedback. Deliver it systematically, with empathy and confidence, using the CARE model. If you're not used to providing feedback, that's okay. Jot down what went well and areas for improvement. Keep practicing, as many people are eager to receive your feedback.

Public recognition: Identify a standout team member who merits praise for their exceptional work. Consider the last time you recognized their contributions. Act now, and plan a moment to celebrate their efforts! Practice giving praise in a group setting to motivate others and encourage colleagues to share in the recognition. Use this method to boost team morale and refine your feedback skills.

"Great leaders understand that feedback isn't merely another task to complete. It serves as the foundation for building trust, enhancing performance, and unlocking potential."

NOTES

NOTES

CHAPTER SIX: THE 6TH PRINCIPLE

ELICITING FEEDBACK

Start a Leadership Revolution with Four Epic Words!

There stands the leader, the one who doesn't bark orders but inspires a wave of ingenuity, commitment, and accountability in every single team member. The secret to this breakthrough event? Four simple but powerful words: "What Do You Think?"

A frustrated senior manager burst into my office not too long ago, steam practically shooting out of his ears. "My team's totally dropping the ball!" he groaned. "I give them clear instructions and hand out tasks, and they still move like snails. Where's the accountability?!" His rant was a classic leadership faux pas, thinking orders alone would light a fire under anyone. I leaned in with a grin and hit him with a question: "What do you want them to feel accountable to?" He fired back, "The tasks I gave them, obviously!"

"Ah, yes, of course," I said. "But here's the thing, people don't rally around tasks—they rally around people. Just listing out goals or tasks doesn't inspire anyone on its own. Real motivation comes from leaders who build strong relationships, where trust and accountability are present. It's that connection to the person, not the task, that drives commitment." I continued, "Do you ever ask your team what they think about the tasks you dish out?" He froze, eyebrows scrunched. "Why would I do that?"

Cue the mic drop: *What do you think?* These four words are a leader's secret weapon. They aren't just a question—they're a high-voltage spark that ignites trust, elevates everyone's voice, and builds rock-solid accountability. When you ask, "What do you think?" you're not merely seeking ideas—you're sending a message that announces: *You're a key player in this adventure!*

In today's world, especially with younger individuals joining the workforce, people strive to have a seat at the cool kids' table. They want to feel seen, heard, and valued. By posing this question, you're rolling out the red carpet for their thoughts, cultivating a culture where trust, connection, and recognition are not the exception—they are the norm.

Feedback is the unsung hero of leadership, the sixth principle that supports a thriving, innovative workplace. Now let's explore the benefits of seeking feedback and outline various opportunities to make it a natural and consistent element of your leadership.

1. The Benefits of Seeking Feedback

When you swing open the door to feedback, you're not just politely nodding and listening—you're unleashing a surge of motivation that can energize your team and transform your organization. Here's why inviting feedback is your secret weapon for success.

Trust Turbocharge

Welcoming input goes far beyond a polite nod or a feel-good gesture—it's a powerful declaration that says, loud and clear, *Your voice matters here.* When leaders and team members truly listen—not just out of obligation, but with curiosity and intention—they create a culture where people feel safe to speak up, challenge ideas, and bring their whole selves to the table.

Genuinely hearing your team lays the foundation for the kind of trust that shows up in every interaction. It's the difference between a team that hesitates and one that moves with confidence. Picture the classic trust fall exercise—but instead of anxious glances and half-hearted catches, everyone's smiling, fully assured that someone's there to catch them every single time. That's what it looks like when trust is real and deeply rooted.

This kind of trust doesn't just appear overnight—it's built over time, through consistent, open dialogue where feedback flows in both directions, and every idea, no matter where it comes from, is treated with respect. When people know their input won't be dismissed or overlooked, they lean in more, contribute freely, and collaborate better.

The outcome is a team that's more than the sum of its parts. A group of individuals transformed into a cohesive, resilient, and unstoppable force—ready to innovate, tackle challenges, and grow together with mutual respect and unwavering support.

Finely Tuned Team

Teams often resemble high-performance machines—complex, powerful, and capable of remarkable things when every part works in sync. In this metaphor, feeling valued isn't just a nice bonus; it's the top-grade oil that keeps everything running smoothly. When people's ideas and efforts are genuinely respected, the entire system operates more efficiently, with less friction and greater momentum.

Actively seeking feedback acts as a catalyst. It fuels connection, sparks collaboration, and keeps the team running like a finely tuned engine. Every member becomes a vital component—seamlessly integrated and moving with precision, purpose, and unity.

With regular check-ins to assess progress (a metaphorical dipstick) and shared celebrations to mark achievements, the team stays aligned and energized. Even the toughest challenges become opportunities for innovation and growth.

Powered by mutual respect, authentic camaraderie, and a well-oiled system of support, this kind of team doesn't just get the job done—they cruise toward success with confidence, leaving behind a trail of accomplishments and a lasting culture of collaboration.

Engagement Explosion

I am always amazed at the positive energy that emerges from employees who see their suggestions shaping their company's mission. These folks don't just show up for another day at the office—they dive in headfirst with enthusiasm and purpose. When employees know that their input directly influences the organization's big picture, it drives action. More than just completing tasks, it's transforming routine work into passionate pursuits that drive progress with a sense of ownership, reshaping their mindset. Employees begin to see that their roles extend beyond their titles and standard duties—they see themselves as essential players in a collective mission. Every idea they propose, every suggestion they voice, becomes a building block in the company's journey. This connection serves as fuel for their motivation, turning standard responsibilities into opportunities to make a meaningful impact.

Growth Accelerator

Feedback isn't always a high five or a pat on the back, and that's exactly what makes it so effective. It serves as a mirror, reflecting not only your strengths but also your blind spots, those areas you may overlook or undervalue. Every piece of constructive input, whether it stings or inspires, acts like a personal trainer for your leadership skills. It pushes you to stretch beyond your comfort zone, refine your approach, and sharpen your decision-making. By embracing feedback, you're not just absorbing advice—you're actively sculpting yourself into a more insightful, adaptable, and effective leader, capable of guiding your team with greater clarity and impact.

Conflict Diffuser

Let's be real, when issues or frustrations go unspoken, they don't just disappear. They lurk beneath the surface, quietly eroding trust, morale, and the team's effectiveness. Over time, that unspoken tension creates an atmosphere where people hold back their ideas, concerns, or even just honest opinions. The team might seem fine on the surface, but underneath, people are second-guessing, avoiding tough conversations, or just going through the motions.

Creating an open feedback culture begins by demonstrating that honest conversations are not only welcome but expected and valued. That could mean regularly asking the team, "What's something we could be doing better?" during meetings, or setting up anonymous feedback tools to help people speak up more freely. It might be as simple as saying, "I know I don't always get it right, let me know what's working for you and what's not," to model vulnerability. Over time, this kind of openness builds trust. When people feel safe while being authentic with each other, it strengthens relationships, improves collaboration, and keeps small problems from becoming major ones. As a leader, when you create space for these conversations and listen and act on what you hear, you're showing that everyone's voice matters.

2. Feedback Opportunities

Creating a workplace where feedback is an integral part of your culture can truly transform things for the better. When your team knows their ideas influence the company's direction, they bring renewed energy and enthusiasm. Seeking feedback offers new perspectives, enhances decision-making, and strengthens collaboration. Here are some strategies to stimulate feedback.

One-on-One Check-Ins

To expand on the concept of creating open communication within a team, consider scheduling private, one-on-one meetings with each team member to create a safe and supportive environment for discussing their work, challenges, and innovative ideas. These individual sessions provide a platform for candid, spontaneous feedback, which is especially valuable for team members who may feel hesitant or uncomfortable sharing their thoughts in group settings. To ensure meaningful dialogue, ask open-ended, thought-provoking questions such as, "What's one thing we could do better as a team?" or "What's a challenge you're facing that I might be able to help with?" These questions invite honest responses and demonstrate your genuine interest in your team members' perspectives.

Drawing from my own experience earlier in my career, I developed a creative and highly effective exercise I called Walk-In Office Hours, inspired by a classic scene from Peanuts where Lucy sets up a booth with a sign that reads The Doctor Is In, inviting Charlie Brown to share his thoughts for a modest fee of five cents. Taking a page from Lucy's playbook, I implemented a structured yet approachable initiative where I posted a physical sign outside my office or workspace that read "Open Feedback Hours: Monday through Wednesday, 9 a.m. to 11 a.m." This sign served as a clear, welcoming invitation for team members to drop by during designated times to discuss anything on their minds, whether it was a work-related challenge, a new idea, or simply a chance to connect.

The key to making your walk-in office hours successful is to create an atmosphere of approachability and active engagement. During these sessions, practice active listening by maintaining eye contact, nodding to show understanding, and asking follow-up questions to dive deeper into the person's concerns or suggestions. For example, if someone mentions a difficulty with a project, you might respond with, "Can you tell me more about what's been challenging?" This not only shows that you value their input but also helps uncover root causes and potential solutions. Additionally, it's crucial to clarify that walk-in office hours are a supplement to, not a replacement for, your existing open-door policy. Make it clear to your team that they are welcome to approach you at any time, even outside these designated hours, to ensure no one feels restricted in seeking your guidance.

This initiative is particularly effective for encouraging participation from those who may be shy, introverted, or hesitant to bother you when you appear busy. The structured time slots and visible sign act as a gentle nudge, signaling that you're not only available but eager to hear from them. To enhance the experience, consider making the setting a bit more inviting by offering coffee, snacks, or heck, even pizza during these hours, which will make the environment feel more relaxed and inviting. Over time, this practice can build stronger relationships, boost team morale, and uncover valuable insights that might otherwise remain unspoken, ultimately contributing to a more cohesive and innovative team dynamic.

Team Brainstorming Sessions

We all know that person who often conjures up truly outstanding ideas. Their ability to think outside the box is nothing short of remarkable, and their contributions are often met with well-deserved praise. But as brilliant as a single mind can be, there's an unparalleled magic that happens when you bring together a group of diverse perspectives.

The real benefits of collective ideas emerge when feedback flows freely from multiple individuals across an organization, each bringing their unique experiences, expertise, and viewpoints to the table. This dynamic exchange of ideas not only adds to the conversation but also multiplies the potential for breakthroughs. When people from different backgrounds and disciplines collaborate, they challenge each other's assumptions, build on one another's strengths, and uncover solutions that might never have surfaced in isolation.

I once had the privilege of participating in a dynamic think tank session designed to explore innovative marketing strategies for a company looking to redefine its brand. The room was buzzing with energy, and while I was eager to contribute several ideas to the discussion, the true magic unfolded through the collaborative efforts of a diverse group of professionals. The session included representatives from human resources, sales, marketing, operations, and to my surprise, engineering, a department not typically involved in marketing brainstorming.

Each participant brought a new perspective shaped by their role in the organization. The HR team highlighted the importance of aligning the campaign with the company's culture and values, ensuring that employees would feel proud to champion the brand. Sales shared insights from customer interactions, revealing pain points and desires that could shape the messaging. Marketing, of course, brought its expertise in storytelling and audience engagement, while operations emphasized the need for strategies that were logistically feasible. The engineers, unexpectedly, offered a tech-driven perspective, suggesting ways to integrate cutting-edge tools like augmented reality into the campaign, an idea that hadn't even crossed my mind.

What made this session so extraordinary was the way these diverse viewpoints didn't just coexist, they intertwined. Ideas were tossed around, dissected, and rebuilt stronger through constructive feedback. A suggestion from one department would encourage a new thought in another, leading to a cascade of innovation. For example, the engineers' augmented reality concept was refined by marketing's storytelling expertise, resulting in an interactive campaign idea that felt both futuristic and deeply human. Meanwhile, operations ensured the plan was grounded in reality, mapping out a timeline and resources to make it happen.

This teamwork across departments didn't just produce ideas— it generated practical, actionable strategies that leveraged everyone's unique strengths. The final concepts were so innovative and well-rounded that they could have left even a solo genius in awe. What started as a simple brainstorming session evolved into a class in collective problem-solving, proving that the sum of a group's vision is far greater than its individual parts.

Organizations that harness the power of diverse collaboration will always have the edge. By creating spaces where varied perspectives can collide and combine, companies can unlock a level of innovation that's not just impressive, it's transformative. So, the next time you're tempted to rely solely on that one brilliant mind, remember: A single flame is compelling, but a collective blaze changes the game.

Anonymous Feedback Channels

Gathering meaningful feedback is crucial for growth, enhancing processes, and building trust within any team or organization. This exercise is one of my absolute favorite methods for doing so, as it consistently delivers results. The approach is simple yet highly effective, leveraging tools like online surveys (SurveyMonkey is my go-to), digital suggestion boxes, or other platforms designed for anonymous input. Anonymity is key here—it removes the fear of judgment or repercussions, which often prevents people from sharing their true thoughts in face-to-face settings. By creating a safe space for honesty, you enable even the most reserved individuals to offer candid and constructive feedback that might otherwise remain unspoken.

For example, consider launching a quarterly feedback campaign with a clear and inviting prompt, such as, "Tell us anonymously: What's working well, and what needs a tweak?" To ensure you're gathering actionable insights, include specific, targeted questions that prompt thoughtful responses. Examples might include "What's one process or workflow that's slowing down your productivity?" or "How can leadership better support you in achieving your goals?" You could also ask, "What's one thing we could start, stop, or continue to improve your work experience?" These types of questions not only result in reflection but also provide concrete feedback that can be analyzed and acted upon.

To maximize participation, make the process as user-friendly as possible. Choose intuitive survey tools such as SurveyMonkey, keep the questionnaire concise, and clearly communicate the purpose to your team. Explain why their input matters and how management will use it to drive positive change. For instance, you might say, "Your feedback will help us identify what's working and where we can improve, ensuring we're all set up for success." Additionally, consider offering multiple channels for feedback, such as a mix of surveys, suggestion boxes, or even anonymous comment forms, to accommodate different preferences and comfort levels. Also, don't forget to make the survey(s) available in multiple languages if necessary.

Equally, if not more, important is what happens after the feedback is collected. Transparency and follow-through are essential to maintaining trust in the process. Once you have gathered the responses, take the time to analyze the data and identify common themes or recurring suggestions. Then, share a high-level summary of the findings with your team, along with a clear action plan outlining how management will address their feedback. For example, if multiple respondents highlight a cumbersome approval process, you might announce, "Based on your input, we're streamlining our approval workflow by implementing a new digital tool next quarter." Even if specific suggestions can't be acted upon immediately, acknowledge them and explain why, so participants feel heard and valued.

By consistently closing the feedback loop in this way, you demonstrate that the process isn't just a formality—it's a meaningful commitment to improvement. Over time, this builds a culture of trust and openness, where team members feel confident to share their perspectives, knowing their voices will make a difference. To maintain momentum, incorporate feedback collection into your team's regular rhythm, whether through quarterly surveys, annual in-depth reviews, or ongoing suggestion channels. This ultimately leads to a more engaged, collaborative, and innovative team that's continuously evolving for the better.

Post-Project Follow-Up

Completing a team project is a significant achievement, but don't let the momentum fade by jumping straight to the next task. Seize the opportunity to gather feedback and reflect on the experience. Conducting a thoughtful post-project review not only establishes engagement but also validates your team's hard work, boosting morale and setting the stage for future success.

Bring your team together shortly after the project wraps up, ideally within a few days, to capture insights while the details are still fresh. Create a safe, open environment where everyone feels comfortable sharing their thoughts. Try asking, "What helped us accomplish our goal here?" and "What would make the next endeavor even smoother?" This collaborative session can uncover valuable lessons, strengthen team dynamics, and refine processes for upcoming endeavors.

Peer-to-Peer Feedback

Encouraging peer-to-peer feedback is one of the best ways to build a team culture rooted in growth, accountability, and genuine collaboration. When team members feel comfortable giving and receiving honest input, it opens the door to better communication and stronger performance, both individually and as a group.

To make this work, it's important to create a structured, supportive space where feedback feels safe and constructive. It's important for leaders to play an active role in guiding the process, helping team members learn how to give feedback clearly and kindly, and how to take it in with an open mind. This kind of support keeps conversations focused, respectful, and productive.

You can kick things off with thoughtful prompts to trigger meaningful reflection and discussion. Try questions like "How did your teammate's contributions help move the project forward?" or "What could we try differently next time to make our work even stronger?" These kinds of questions celebrate what's working while gently nudging the team to think ahead and look for ways to improve.

As a facilitator, keeping the tone balanced is key. A little lightness, some well-placed humor, or an icebreaker can go a long way in helping people feel more at ease. Just be sure the humor fits your team's style and the moment. Chapter 3 has tips on how to create that balance.

When peer feedback happens in an environment built on trust, respect, and a bit of lightheartedness, it becomes much more than a box to check, it becomes a powerful driver of learning, growth, and better teamwork.

Engagement During Transition

Change can often feel overwhelming for many individuals, stirring unease or even resistance. This pushback typically stems from three primary sources:

- Uncertainty about the tangible benefits the change will bring

- A sense of being sidelined or excluded from the decision-making process

- A lack of confidence in the individual spearheading the transition

Navigating change isn't easy for anyone. That's why gathering feedback during times of transition is so important. It's not just about checking a box—it's about creating a space where people feel heard, supported, and involved. When you invite honest input, you're sending a clear message: *This change isn't being handed down like a top-down decree, it's something we're working through together.*

To make that feedback meaningful, ask thoughtful, open-ended questions, like "How is this change affecting you personally?" or "What support would help you adapt more smoothly?" These kinds of questions invite real, personal responses and show you're genuinely interested in people's experiences. Along with one-on-one conversations, consider using short surveys or informal group chats to get a fuller picture of how your team is feeling and what roadblocks they might be facing.

Just as important: Act on what you hear. When people see that their feedback leads to actual changes, or at least thoughtful consideration, they're far more likely to stay engaged, even when things get tough.

Of course, not every concern can be accommodated. In those cases, how you respond makes all the difference. Here's how to handle that with care.

1. Acknowledge the concern with respect: Even if you can't fix the issue, take the time to validate the person's perspective. Say something like "I know this change is tough," or "Thanks for being honest, I really appreciate you speaking up." This kind of acknowledgment goes a long way in building trust and showing that you're listening.

2. Be honest about what's possible: If a concern can't be acted on, explain why. Maybe it's due to company priorities, resource limits, or factors outside your control. Whatever the reason, being upfront helps people feel respected and included, even when the answer isn't what they hoped for.

3. Connect to the bigger picture: When it makes sense, help people see how the change ties into broader goals or values. Framing it this way can help them understand where their work fits in and why certain decisions are necessary, even if they're difficult.

The goal isn't to eliminate all discomfort—that's rarely possible during change—but to show that you're leading with empathy, transparency, and a commitment to ongoing support. In the end, when people feel heard and respected, even when their concerns can't be fully addressed, they're more likely to stay engaged, adaptable, and collaborative. And that kind of trust doesn't just help you get through change, it helps your team grow stronger because of it.

3. Tips for Eliciting Feedback Effectively

Be Specific

Vague questions lead to ambiguous answers. Questions like "What's up?" are like throwing a dart at a blank wall—you're not aiming at anything specific, so you won't hit much. Instead, aim for precision. Ask things like "What's one thing we could tweak to make our weekly meetings less of a snooze-fest and more interesting?" or "What's a tool or process you think our team could use to level up?" Specific questions provide a clear runway for people to share meaningful input. Plus, they demonstrate that you've thought carefully about what you're asking, which makes people more likely to engage. If you have the time, prepare your questions to include anticipated responses. This will ensure a smooth-flowing conversation. Here is an example of what that preparation might look like.

Prepared question: "What's one part of our current project workflow that feels unnecessary or slows you down?"

First anticipated response: "I think the daily stand-up meetings are too long and sometimes repetitive."

Follow-up: "What do you think would make them more efficient: shorter updates, fewer attendees, or maybe switching to written check-ins?"

Second anticipated response: "There are too many approval layers before we can move forward with small decisions."

Follow-up: "Can you point to a recent example where this caused delays? What would an ideal approval process look like to you?"

Third anticipated response: "Our task management tool feels clunky and hard to navigate."

Follow-up: "What features are missing or getting in your way? Is there another tool you've used that you found more effective?"

By preparing specific, open-ended questions along with possible responses and follow-ups, you can keep conversations focused, engaging, and productive, while also showing that you value the input being shared.

Let's pause for a moment. I don't want to assume everyone knows what open-ended questions are. Simply put, an open-ended question is meant to encourage a more detailed response, not just a one-word answer.

Examples of closed-ended questions:

- Do you like working from home?
- Did you go to college?
- Is the project finished?

Examples of open-ended questions:

- What are your thoughts on remote work?
- How did you prepare for the interview?
- Why do you think the project failed?

Using open-ended questions offers a range of valuable benefits in communication, learning, and problem-solving, and is critical when eliciting feedback. Okay, let's move forward.

Create a Safe Zone

People often hold back from sharing honest feedback because they're afraid it might upset someone, cause tension, or even put their job at risk. This is especially true in environments where there's a clear hierarchy, like a workplace where power dynamics are at play. Picture someone in a meeting who spots a flaw in their manager's idea but chooses to stay quiet. Maybe they've spoken up before and were met with defensiveness or brushed off. That kind of experience can stick, and over time it creates an atmosphere where people play it safe, offering surface-level comments or staying silent altogether. This often results in missed opportunities for growth, better ideas, and real improvement.

To break down that fear, it's essential to create a space where people feel genuinely safe speaking up. That starts with setting the tone early. Lay out clear ground rules before any feedback session—make it known that all input is welcome, that there are anonymous ways to share thoughts if needed, and most importantly, that there won't be any negative consequences for being honest. Use simple prompts to open things up, like "What's one thing we did well, and one thing we could improve on?" These kinds of questions help make feedback feel normal, constructive, and part of how your team grows together.

Practical Tips

Model vulnerability: Leaders should share their own self-critiques first, showing it's okay to admit flaws. "Last quarter, I dropped the ball on communication—how can we improve that together?"

Use anonymous tools: Platforms like Google Forms, SurveyMonkey, or even simple suggestion boxes can encourage honesty without the spotlight.

Positive follow-up: After feedback is shared, thank participants publicly and focus on solutions rather than blame. This reinforces that criticism is a tool for collective success, not personal attacks.

By consistently applying these, you'll shift the culture from one of caution to one of collaboration, where feedback flows freely.

Act on It

When people share ideas or critiques, they're giving you a piece of their brainpower. If you ignore it, they'll stop sharing. So, act on what you hear whenever possible. If someone suggests shorter meetings, try a twenty-minute huddle next week and give them a shout-out: "Heads up everyone. Thanks to Brenda's idea, we're keeping this short!" If a suggestion can't happen, like, say, their dream of a Ping-Pong table in the break room doesn't fit the budget, don't dismiss the idea. Instead, explain why: "I love the Ping-Pong concept, but we're saving up for new laptops this quarter. Let's revisit in a few months!" Showing you've heard and considered their input keeps the feedback loop alive. Nothing says, *I value you* like action, or at least a thoughtful response.

Mix It Up

Heads up, my fellow leaders: Not everyone shares feedback in the same way, and that's something worth paying attention to. People are wired differently—some thrive in the intimacy of one-on-one conversations, where they can speak freely without an audience. Others feel more comfortable slipping anonymous notes into a suggestion box, letting their thoughts flow without the spotlight. Then there are those who only really open up in a group setting, tossing ideas around during a lively brainstorming session, ideally with a whiteboard, some Post-its, and a bowl of snacks to keep the energy going.

To truly hear from everyone, you've got to mix up your feed-back methods to suit all personalities, from the introspective introverts to the outspoken extroverts. Rotating your approach does more than just keep things innovative—it prevents feedback fatigue, shakes up the routine, and ensures you're not stuck hearing the same voices over and over again. Variety is key to unlocking insights from every corner of your team, whether it's the quiet thinker who's been sitting on a game-changing idea or the chatty go-getter who's ready to pitch theirs at a moment's notice. By diversifying how you gather input, you create a space where everyone feels invited to contribute, and that's when the real magic happens.

Model It

All right, it's time to step up and lead by example once more. Show your team how it's done by sharing your own constructive feedback in a professional and approachable manner. For instance, during a team meeting, you could say, "I've noticed our monthly reports could benefit from stronger visuals to make the data pop. I experimented with some new chart designs last quarter, and they really helped clarify our key metrics. Here's what I tried." By offering a specific suggestion alongside a personal example, you're not just pointing out an issue but also contributing to the solution.

Then, take it a step further by being transparent with how you've grown from the feedback you've received. You might share: "A couple of months ago, Jennifer gave me some great advice about our meeting agendas. She pointed out that I was packing them with too many topics, which was overwhelming the team. I took her feedback to heart and trimmed the agendas to focus on what matters most. It's made our discussions so much more productive and focused." By openly discussing your own growth, you're not just talking the talk, you're walking the walk, showing that feedback is a valuable two-way street.

This kind of vulnerability and openness does more than set a good example—it creates a safe space for others to share their thoughts without fear of judgment. Before long, your team will be bouncing ideas and constructive critiques off each other like they're playing a lively game of feedback cornhole at a company picnic. That's when you know you've built a culture where everyone feels empowered to contribute and grow together.

Overcoming the Barriers

Gathering meaningful feedback can be challenging. But fear not! By addressing common barriers directly with simple strategies, you can transform reluctant responders into enthusiastic contributors. Below, I'll expand on a couple of barriers and strategies.

Barrier: Lack of trust

Trust issues can turn feedback sessions into a game of hot potato, where people dodge directness to avoid perceived risks. When relationships feel fragile, responses become guarded, vague, or overly polite. This might present as "Everything's fine" when it's not, or cryptic comments that require detective work to unpack. The root cause of these issues can be traced to inconsistent leadership, unresolved conflicts, or a history of broken promises, which leads people to doubt that feedback will be handled fairly. In remote or hybrid teams, this barrier intensifies due to limited face-to-face interactions, making it more challenging to read nonverbal cues and build rapport.

Strategy: Establish or rebuild trust

As highlighted in Chapter 1, trust is the bedrock of effective communication. It starts with consistent, transparent actions that demonstrate your investment in people's growth. Regular one-on-one check-ins aren't just small talk—they're opportunities to listen actively, to ask open-ended questions like "What do you think about our processes?" and to demonstrate genuine empathy. Over time, this creates a feedback loop where trust builds upon itself.

Practical Tips

Be consistent and reliable: Make good on small commitments to demonstrate dependability. For instance, if someone recommends a tool, test it out and share your feedback. This promotes trust and invites input when opportunities arise.

Encourage two-way streets: Make feedback bidirectional by soliciting input on your own performance as a leader or colleague, creating a sense of equality. This can be done openly or anonymously—either approach will work, but be sure to follow up and share your perspectives.

Build personal connections: In team settings, incorporate team-building activities, virtual coffee chats, or shared goals to humanize interactions. For instance, starting meetings with nonwork shares like "What's a win from your week?" can warm up the room.

Address breaches head-on: Tackle issues head-on to rebuild trust and keep things moving: If trust has taken a hit, maybe from miscommunication, missed expectations, or outside pressures, be upfront about it. Skip the defensiveness and address it openly from the start. Being genuine like this sets the tone for honest conversations and encourages others to speak up as well.

You could say something like "I know the recent changes didn't go as smoothly as they should have, and I take responsibility for that. It's thrown off our team's rhythm, and I'm sorry. But I'd like us to move forward together, starting with your thoughts on what we need to get right."

Once you've acknowledged the issue, shift quickly into action: Get the team involved in fixing it. Set up brainstorming sessions or anonymous feedback channels so everyone has a chance to contribute. Not only does this help repair the situation, but it also gives the team ownership, turning a setback into something that strengthens trust, teamwork, and innovation in the long run.

Barrier: Low perceived value

Nothing kills motivation faster than feeling like your voice echoes into a void. When people believe their feedback won't lead to change—perhaps because past suggestions gathered dust in a forgotten inbox—they disengage quickly. This perception arises from a lack of visibility into how input is utilized, or when changes occur without proper credit being given. It's like shouting into the wind: Why bother if it doesn't make a difference? This barrier is common in large organizations where bureaucracy slows implementation, or in stressful environments where feedback gets lost amid competing priorities, ultimately leading to apathy and reduced innovation.

Strategy: Act on feedback

The antidote is visibility and accountability: Turn feedback into tangible outcomes and broadcast them to close the loop. This not only validates contributors but also inspires ongoing participation by showing that every voice counts. For example, after collecting input on workflow inefficiencies, implement a quick win, such as streamlining a meeting agenda, announcing, "Thanks to your suggestions, we've cut our weekly meetings by fifteen minutes, and here's how it helps."

Prioritize and categorize: Sort feedback into short-term (quick fixes), medium-term (projects), and long-term (strategic shifts) categories to manage expectations effectively. Use tools to track progress publicly.

Communicate progress regularly: Send updates via emails or newsletters. Wording like "Your idea on flexible hours is now in pilot. Stay tuned for results," keeps the momentum going.

Celebrate contributions: Recognize individuals or groups in team shout-outs, awards, or even small perks, reinforcing that input drives impact.

Call to Action

When you're ready to start cultivating a culture of feedback in your workplace, select one method that best suits your team, whether it's a quick pulse survey, a dedicated team meeting, an anonymous suggestion box, or even casual one-on-one check-ins. The key is to act to implement your chosen method this week.

Make it official by announcing it to your team with enthusiasm: "I'm excited to kick off a new program designed to gather your thoughts and ideas. Let's collaborate to make our workplace truly unstoppable!"

To ensure success, establish clear goals for collecting and utilizing feedback. Share a straightforward timeline with your team so they know what to expect.

As responses come in, diligently monitor progress and demonstrate your commitment by acting on the input you receive, whether it's implementing a small change or addressing a larger concern. Communicate updates regularly to keep everyone informed.

By consistently valuing and acting on feedback, you will create an environment where trust, innovation, and engagement shine, unlocking your team's full potential.

*"The goal isn't to eliminate all discomfort—
that's rarely possible during change—but
to show that you're leading with empathy,
transparency, and a commitment
to ongoing support."*

NOTES

NOTES

CHAPTER SEVEN: THE 7TH PRINCIPLE

EMPATHY

Back when I was booking consulting and speaking gigs regularly, I became quite the LinkedIn enthusiast, consistently sharing content on leadership, culture, teamwork, and humor. I thought I'd seen it all until my son, Mason, stole the show with a story that blew up my feed like nothing else. six years ago, I shared a post called "A Lesson in Empathy from a Ten-Year-Old," and it struck a nerve, garnering thousands of reactions.

A Lesson in Empathy from a Ten-Year-Old

Mason, my little money-hoarder, was *the* king of frugality. The kid saved every penny like it was his job! But a couple years ago on his tenth birthday, he hit me with a curveball. "Dad," he said, "I wanna spend some of my money." I was thinking, *YES! Finally, we're hitting the toy store or snagging some epic gear!* So

I asked, "What's the plan, buddy?" And this kid, this absolute legend, said, "Can we go to McDonald's, buy a bunch of lunches, and stuff the back of your Jeep with them?" (I had just finished restoring a 1979 Jeep CJ5, a true beauty.)

I was like, "Uh, I'm not sure I follow Mason, what do you mean?" Then he hit me with this: He wanted to cruise around town and hand out those meals to people on the streets, holding signs. I blink, processing, and say, "You want to spend your hard-saved loot on lunches for panhandlers?" He nodded, all serious, and asked, "Is that okay?" I was choking back a tear, trying to play it cool, and managed to croak out, "Yeah, son, it's more than okay, it's awesome."

So we hit the road, McDonald's bags piled high, and spent hours driving around, spreading joy. We had to restock three times! Mason's face lit up every time someone smiled over a hot meal. He didn't ask their names, didn't dig into their stories, didn't judge their situations. He just gave, pure and simple. And get this: To this day, he's never bragged about it. Not once. He wasn't looking for recognition—he didn't need or even want anyone to know of his generosity. That, my friends, is empathy with a capital E.

A Key Trait for Leadership

When folks ask me, "Are leaders born or made?" I always grin and say, "Nope, no such thing as a natural-born leader!" Leadership isn't some mystical gift dropped from the heavens—however, some people *are* born with a knack for the traits that make leadership shine. And if there's one trait that deserves a standing ovation, it's empathy.

Empathy is the hidden strength that makes leaders truly legendary! It's like having the ability to dive into someone else's universe, genuinely understand where they're coming from, grasp their highs, and feel their lows, all while shouting, "I've got your back, let's roll!" Forget a quick "Wow, that's rough" or half-hearted nod. Empathy is truly tuning in to what inspires your team or what's quietly weighing them down.

Now, before we dive any deeper into this topic, I want to pause for a second and speak to something that has tripped up many folks I've spoken to over the years: the all-too-common mix-up between empathy and sympathy. It's one of those distinctions that sounds simple on paper, but in the heat of everyday interactions, they can blur together. Let me break it down for you step by step, because getting this right can transform how you connect with people, whether it's a close friend, a colleague, or even a stranger who just doesn't feel right.

First off, sympathy is that initial, surface-level acknowledgment we all turn to when someone's going through a rough patch. Here's an example: You're at work, and your teammate pulls up to the morning meeting looking a little hollow-eyed, then drops the news that their beloved dog passed away unexpectedly over the weekend. You say, "Aw, man, that absolutely stinks—I'm so sorry you're dealing with this." It's a heartfelt nod to their pain, perhaps even a quick hug that says you've heard them and you care enough to respond with kindness. Sympathy doesn't demand you dive into the emotional deep end. You're simply validating their feelings without necessarily pulling yourself into the details. It's polite, it's human, and it's a solid starting point for showing you notice someone's hurting.

But empathy? Oh, that's where things get truly powerful, it's sympathy's more intuitive sibling, the one that doesn't wait for an invitation or a full confession to step up. Empathy kicks in like an internal radar, picking up on those quiet signals that others might miss entirely. You don't need the dramatic backstory, the waterworks, or even a single word from them to sense it. Maybe it's that barely perceptible slump in their shoulders as they scroll through their phone during lunch, or the way their laugh rings a touch too hollow in a group chat. No prying questions, no snap judgments, just a quiet recognition that something's weighing on them. And from there, empathy propels you to act, not out of obligation but from a place of shared humanity. You slide over with a casual coffee refill and a low-key comment, like "Hey, rough day? I've got your back. You want to vent or just sit with it?" It's that unspoken message: *I see you, I feel the echo of this with you, and we're navigating it side by side, no solo journeys here.*

The beauty of empathy lies in its proactive nature—it builds bridges, establishing trust and resilience in relationships that sympathy alone might overlook. The next time you notice a subtle shift in someone's energy, lean in with empathy. The goal is not to fix their problems, but to be a steady ally in the midst of it all.

With that cleared up, let's keep rolling.

Consider the seventh principle as the essential support for your heart, guiding your emotions and nurturing your capacity for compassion. On this journey, I encourage you to set aside all preconceptions, adopt a perspective free of bias, and engage with the world with eyes wide open and a heart ready to connect deeply with others.

Let's begin with identifying the many values of leading with empathy, a timeless yet increasingly vital approach in today's diverse workplaces. Empathy, at its core, involves understanding and sharing the feelings of others, allowing leaders to connect on a human level rather than just directing from a distance. Far from being just a soft skill, it drives tangible outcomes that enhance organizational success. Below, I'll expand on key values to illustrate why empathetic leadership isn't just nice, it's essential.

Forges Undeniable Trust

When your team feels genuinely understood, heart, soul, and everything in between, they'll rally behind you with unwavering trust and loyalty, ready to follow your lead through any challenge. Empathy is the ultimate key! It creates a supportive, inclusive environment where your people are celebrated as the unique and passionate individuals they truly are. By leading with empathy, you promote a deep sense of belonging and purpose. A glance in the rearview mirror reveals a motivated, cohesive team, fully committed and eager to charge toward your shared vision, no matter where the journey takes you!

Inspires Vision and Courage

Imagine stepping into a workplace where your most outside-the-box ideas aren't just tolerated, they're celebrated and catapulted into groundbreaking realities. Wouldn't that inspire you? Absolutely. That's the magic of empathy in action. Exceptional leaders don't merely nod along—they dive deep into your world with genuine curiosity and compassion. They listen intently, not as a formality but as a bridge to true understanding, tuning in to your unique viewpoint with both an open heart and a razor-sharp intellect.

This connection goes far beyond surface-level conversations. The objective is to create a safe space where vulnerability meets innovation, where your quirks and hunches are met with encouragement rather than skepticism. These leaders champion your voice, asking probing questions that unlock hidden layers of possibility: "What if we flipped this entirely?" or "How might this challenge the status quo?" In doing so, they enable you to shatter conventions, experiment, and embrace the thrill of calculated risks.

With their steady support turning your mistakes into chances to grow, you're not just allowed to dream, you're pushed to make things happen. This kind of encouragement taps into your true creative energy. Their rock-solid belief in you wipes away doubts and ignites big, brave goals. All at once, you're thinking big, dreaming without limits, and building legacies that change what's possible. In their circle, vision is the fuel for real progress and courage. It's just what happens when someone truly sees and trusts you.

Navigating Leadership Challenges

In today's unpredictable world, leadership is an endeavor that requires resilience. Leaders frequently struggle with a cascade of challenges, including interpersonal conflicts that can erode trust, unforeseen setbacks, and the weight of making high-impact decisions under intense time pressure and incomplete information. These challenges not only test strategic acumen but also emotional resolve, demanding a delicate balance between action and restraint.

What sets exceptional leaders apart is their shift from mere authority figures to empathetic navigators of human dynamics. Rather than relying solely on issuing directives or enforcing top-down mandates, they cultivate a deep understanding of their team—the quiet frustrations bubbling beneath the surface, the unvoiced aspirations for growth, and the subtle fears that uncertainty can amplify. Empathy isn't performative—it's a deliberate practice rooted in genuine curiosity about the people they lead.

Ultimately, empathetic leadership transforms potential pitfalls into opportunities for unity. It mitigates escalating tensions before they fracture relationships, steering the collective energy toward shared objectives with renewed purpose. In doing so, it doesn't just help you weather adversity—it forges a resilient, cohesive environment where individuals feel seen, valued, and empowered to contribute their best, turning challenges into the very foundation of enduring success.

A Magnet for Loyalty

One of the most frequently asked questions I receive from leaders is: "How do you hire employees who are truly loyal?" My response never wavers: "It's impossible to simply hire loyalty outright." Loyalty isn't some fixed personality trait you can screen for in a résumé or interview (although I wish we could)—it's an organic outcome that emerges over time, much like trust in any relationship. Instead of chasing it as a prerequisite, the real key lies in nurturing it deliberately within your team.

To develop a group of devoted professionals who'll stand by you during the highs and lows of business life, begin at the foundation: Lead with authentic care and empathy. Great leaders don't merely assemble a roster of talent—they weave together tight-knit communities where every individual feels profoundly valued and intertwined with the group's purpose. Imagine showing your team members, not through empty words but through consistent actions, that they are indispensable not only to the company's grand mission but also to you on a personal level. Treat them as irreplaceable partners, far beyond the role of interchangeable cogs in a machine.

When people sense this level of genuine investment in their growth, well-being, and contributions, something remarkable happens. They pour their passion and energy into the work, forging a deep emotional commitment that endures beyond paychecks or perks.

What starts as professional dedication evolves into a bond that elevates the workplace team from a mere group of colleagues into a supportive family, resilient against challenges and fueled by mutual respect. In the end, this cultivated loyalty becomes your greatest asset, a magnetic force that attracts and retains the best, ensuring your vision thrives for the long haul.

The 2021 Ernst & Young *Empathy in Business Survey* of about a thousand US workers revealed just how powerful empathy can be in the workplace. Eighty-seven percent of employees said that when their leaders show genuine empathy, it not only makes them more satisfied with their jobs—it also helps build stronger trust between employees and leadership.7 That trust isn't just a warm, fuzzy feeling—it's a critical piece of what keeps teams motivated and connected.

On the flip side, the same survey showed the damage that a lack of empathy can cause. More than half of the respondents (54 percent) said they had left a job because their boss didn't show understanding around work-related challenges, and nearly as many (49 percent) said the same when it came to personal struggles. When leaders fail to show empathy, employees feel unsupported and disconnected, and that can seriously undermine trust—and push good people out the door.

Clearly, empathy isn't just a nice-to-have—it's a leadership essential. But that raises a fair question: Is empathy something you can actually build, or are some people just naturally better at it than others?

Let's dive back into the heartwarming story of my son Mason. This kid, with his boundless compassion and big heart, turned a simple act of kindness into a viral moment of inspiration.

When I shared Mason's story on LinkedIn, expecting maybe a few likes and a "that's sweet" comment or two, the internet practically exploded with awe. The comments rolled in: "Is it his upbringing?" and "Did you teach him this?" Suddenly, Mason wasn't just my son—he was a beacon of hope who'd stumbled into the spotlight simply by being his big-hearted self.

So, what's the secret behind Mason's gift? I've given this a lot of thought, and I believe it's a mix of nature, nurture, and a touch of something unexplainable. He's always been curious about people's stories, asking questions like, "Why's that man sitting on the sidewalk?" instead of looking away. We've advised him to listen, to feel, and to act when he can. But the brilliance? That's all him. It's in the way he shines when he hands someone a hot meal or how he'll spend his last dollar to brighten someone else's day. It's not just generosity—it's a deep, soul-level understanding that we're all connected.

People keep asking, "How can we raise kids like him?" My answer? Let them see the world, let them care, and don't be surprised when they show you up. Sure, some folks might come out of the womb with an extra dose of emotional radar, those people who just understand how others feel, but there is good news: Empathy can be learned, honed, and polished.

Let's take a look at a few simple strategies designed to ensure you lead with empathy.

Ears On, Distractions Off

Active listening is making its grand return, and it's ready to take center stage. Picture yourself as a detective, intently listening to a witness recount clues that could crack the case wide open. This is more than just hearing words—it's diving deep into the conversation. Resist that itching urge to jump in with your own two cents—seriously, zip your lips and let the speaker take the spotlight. Their words deserve the complete red-carpet treatment, so give them the space to shine.

To show you're truly dialed in, add some curious, temperature-checking questions that prove you're hanging on every detail. Try something like, "Whoa, hold the phone, tell me more! Sounds like this project has you jumping through hoops." Not only does this keep the conversation flowing but it also signals you're not just passively nodding like a bobblehead—you're genuinely invested. Keep your tone warm and your energy casual to set the stage for a back-and-forth that feels effortless and alive.

Step into Their World

Slip into your team's favorite pair of shoes, whether they're sneakers, boots, or flip-flops, to truly grasp what drives them: their passions, their challenges, and the moments that ignite their enthusiasm. Building stronger connections begins with initiating open, engaging conversations that feel natural and fun. Try tossing out questions like "What's your take on this?" "What's been firing you up lately?" or even "If you could tackle one thing your way, what would it be?" These kinds of prompts aren't just icebreakers—they're invitations for authentic, heartfelt sharing that demonstrate you're genuinely attuned. By listening closely and responding with curiosity, you create a space where empathy, trust, and collaboration can excel. This approach transforms your team into a group where everyone feels heard, valued, and energized to bring their best ideas and energy to the table every day.

Connect Deeply

To forge a deep connection, focus on understanding someone's emotional world with empathy and sincerity. Offer a heartfelt response like "I can feel how heavy this is for you," to affirm their emotions and show you're present with them in their struggle. Let me emphasize that again, because I truly feel this captures the essence of empathy: *Show you're present with them in their struggle.* Spot-on!

Avoid brushing off their worries, dismissing their feelings, or jumping to fix things. Instead, provide an opportunity to share openly. Listen attentively, remaining fully present without interrupting or redirecting the conversation. Ensure they feel heard, respected, and valued before even considering suggesting solutions. This builds trust, strengthens your bond, and allows them to feel supported and understood in their own way.

Get Real, Get Vulnerable

In a world obsessed with picture-perfect lives, there's something refreshingly authentic about revealing your true self. Dropping the mask and sharing a genuine moment, like missing a deadline or struggling with self-doubt, makes you instantly more relatable. It's like saying, "Hey, I'm human, too!" and inviting others to connect with the real you.

Being vulnerable doesn't mean sharing your entire life story or venting constantly. It simply means embracing your quirks and missteps with a smile and a shrug. For example, if you're stuck on a project, instead of pretending you have it all together, you say, "I'm kinda lost here, got any ideas?" Boom! You've just shown you're human, opened the door to teamwork, and made it okay for everyone to be a work in progress. That's the benefit of a little honesty.

Letting go of the "what will they think?" fear is incredibly freeing. Everyone has their own struggles, and when you share a slice of yours, like admitting you're juggling work and life like a circus act, you give others the green light to open up, too. One brave moment in a meeting can create a chain reaction of genuine conversation, transforming a group into a cohesive and supportive team. Empathy in motion!

Celebrate the Mosaic

Building a welcoming team culture starts with appreciating the different backgrounds, experiences, and ways of communicating that everyone brings to the table. Think of your team like a colorful mosaic—each person's story, culture, and journey adds something unique to the bigger picture. When you listen with empathy, you help people feel seen, heard, and valued.

Take the time to learn about your teammates' perspectives with curiosity and an open mind. Invite them to share their traditions, ideas, and experiences in a space that feels safe and free of judgment. Keep it optional, but make sure everyone feels included. Listen not just to respond, but to truly connect—and let empathy help you see things from their perspective. That kind of connection helps close gaps and makes sure everyone has a voice. And mix in fun team activities, casual chats, or light workshops that highlight each person's individuality. These shared moments can ease tensions, build trust, and turn coworkers into a strong, supportive team. Encourage questions, laugh together, and keep it light—it's all part of creating a space where people feel like they truly belong.

Overcoming the Barriers

Whether innate or cultivated, embracing empathy as a foundational leadership skill can present specific challenges, from emotional exhaustion to resistance, in stressful environments. Let's examine practical strategies to overcome these common barriers.

Barrier: Time pressure and workload

When you're leading a team, getting buried under deadlines and a nonstop workload is one of the toughest roadblocks to building real empathy. You're usually bouncing between a million urgent things: endless meetings, big-picture calls, handling crises, running reviews, and keeping everyone in the loop. It all adds up to this frantic pace where every second feels spoken for, and "do it quick" becomes the only rule that matters.

In that kind of rush, empathy, like actually stopping to hear out your team's take, their frustrations, or what's stressing them personally, starts to feel like a side quest. It can seem too touchy-feely, vague, or even a bit selfish, especially in comparison to the tasks that demand attention, such as meeting quarterly numbers or resolving a glitch that's holding everything up.

Strategy: Make empathy a low-effort habit

This involves reframing it as a tool for efficiency, embedding small practices into daily routines, and leveraging existing structures to amplify its impact without increasing your workload. Here's a step-by-step guide.

Audit and prioritize your current schedule: Begin by spending ten minutes scanning your daily or weekly calendar, maybe while commuting or in a quiet moment. Spot recurring activities, such as one-on-one check-ins, group stand-ups, or email threads, where you can naturally incorporate empathy without tacking on extra time. For example, during an existing thirty-minute progress review with a team member, dedicate the opening two minutes to a simple open-ended prompt like "What's one hurdle you're tackling this week?" It builds rapport seamlessly, no additional time slots required.

Empathetic framing in emails: When assigning tasks via email, especially in high-pressure environments, a simple empathetic acknowledgment can transform a directive from cold instruction to collaborative encouragement. For instance, instead of just saying, "Please handle the Q3 report by Friday," try framing it like this: "I know the team has been under a lot of pressure with the recent deadlines, so I truly appreciate you taking this on. Let's get the Q3 report wrapped up by Friday."

This approach humanizes your message by validating the recipient's workload, promoting goodwill and reducing resentment. It takes mere seconds to add yet boosts response rates and team morale.

Daily check-ins using available tools: To create a supportive work environment, especially during high-pressure periods, I make it a habit to integrate brief daily check-ins using platforms like Microsoft Teams. These typically happen at the start of my day to set a positive tone without disrupting workflows. For instance, I might call someone on a face-to-face call (this helps me gauge their body language) and say: "Hey, I know you've been juggling several new projects this week, so I just wanted to check in on how you're doing and see if you need any support, whether it's brainstorming ideas, reallocating resources, or just venting about a deadline."

I incorporate these ten-minute check-ins regularly with my team leaders and direct reports, tailoring the frequency based on individual needs: a few times a week for those in crunch mode, once a week for others. What I've found is that in just a few minutes, they often uncover small but critical issues while strengthening the relationship with empathy and, yes, a bit of humor as well.

Barrier: Emotional burnout

Burnout is a huge roadblock for leaders trying to build empathy in their teams. Basically, it's that constant feeling of being wiped out, physically and emotionally, from dealing with stress nonstop. For leaders, it hits hard because of the endless decisions, juggling priorities, and owning the team's wins and losses. When it comes to empathy, really getting where someone's coming from and responding with care, burnout throws a wrench in it. Your emotional energy is shot, so it's tough to put yourself in others' shoes or tune in to their feelings. Imagine a leader who's fried: They might brush off a team member's issue as no big deal instead of digging in, which chips away at trust and team spirit. You see this all the time in stressful industries like tech or healthcare, where bosses admit they're numb to their people's struggles during crunch times or crises, which negatively affects collaboration and new ideas.

Strategy: Supercharge self-care

Think of it as fueling up your leadership tank: not some fancy add-on, but a smart move to stay sharp and real with your team. This isn't just crashing on the couch—it's developing smart, proven habits that build your bounce-back power and emotional resilience, so you show up stronger. Here's how to make it happen.

1. Quick mindfulness hits: At the beginning of your workday, or right before a meeting, do just three minutes of deep breathing. Now I realize this may seem a bit basic, but it genuinely dials down stress by activating your body's relaxation response, leaving you less irritable and more focused. I've chatted with executives who've adopted this habit, and they say it sharpens their ability to read their team's cues while keeping a cool, composed demeanor.

2. Get moving to recharge: Aim for thirty minutes of exercise, three to five days a week. It can be jogging, yoga, weights, or whatever floats your boat. Exercise releases endorphins, a feel-good chemical, in your brain and at the same time reduces stress chemicals. This will aid tremendously in fighting burnout, while improving your mood and flexibility, making you more empathetic. Pressed for time? Sneak in a brisk walk midday for a quick recharge.

3. Smart pauses and unplug rituals: In our always-on world, building in intentional breaks shouldn't be a luxury—it's a necessity for sustained productivity and mental clarity. Start by incorporating smart pauses: Schedule mini breaks of just five minutes every hour to step away from your desk, stretch, or simply take a few deep breaths.

If you're hosting a virtual meeting that feels like it's dragging on forever, keep your audience's sanity in mind and show some mercy. Take a five-minute timeout so they can stretch, snack, or gaze at something other than your face. These speedy pit stops ward off total exhaustion, crank up the concentration, and dodge that classic zombie mode where folks are squinting at the screen with one eye half-shut, trudging their way to the bitter end.

For deeper recovery, embrace unplugging rituals that create clear boundaries between work and life. For instance, commit to ditching all screens after a set time, say 8 p.m., and replace scrolling with a calming activity like reading a book or taking a short walk. Establish firm rules, such as no email checks after 7 p.m. or silencing notifications during family dinners, to signal the end of your workday and allow your brain to fully recharge.

The effect is powerful: By modeling these habits, you're not only prioritizing your own well-being but also making it the standard for your team. This creates a workplace culture rooted in understanding, kindness, and empathy, where colleagues feel empowered to step back without guilt. Over time, these small shifts can transform exhaustion into equilibrium, proving that true efficiency comes from balance, not constant grind.

Barrier: Fear of appearing soft

In leadership roles, one of the most common hurdles to embracing empathy is the deep-seated worry that it might make you look weak or overly accommodating. This fear often stems from a belief that vulnerability invites exploitation, turning a strength into a liability. Let me share a personal story that illustrates this.

A few years ago, I delivered a keynote on empathy as a key leadership competency, explaining how it fosters trust, drives innovation, and enhances team performance. As the session wrapped up, a senior executive in the audience raised her hand with a pointed question: "So, at what point do you cross the line and become too nice?" I paused, sensing the weight behind her words, and asked her to elaborate. She opened up about her experiences: In her view, moments of niceness had led subordinates to slack off, miss deadlines, or push boundaries without consequence. It was a raw admission, echoing a sentiment I'd heard from countless leaders across industries.

What struck me most wasn't the question itself, but the underlying assumption. It revealed a widespread misconception that kindness is inherently risky. In reality, people don't exploit you because you're kind—they do so because they've been enabled to believe they can get away with it.

Without clear boundaries, empathy can blur into permissiveness, allowing opportunists to test limits. This barrier isn't just personal—it's cultural, reinforced by outdated notions of leadership as stoic command-and-control. Yet, ignoring it means missing out on empathy's true power: creating loyal, high-performing teams.

Strategy: Be kind, but draw clear lines

The antidote to this fear lies in a simple yet profound shift: Kindness without clarity is incomplete. If someone on your team perceives your attempt at empathy as weakness, address it head-on, but with the very grace you're defending. Start by reframing the narrative in a one-on-one conversation. Approach it calmly and supportively, perhaps over coffee or a quick check-in, to keep the tone collaborative rather than confrontational.

1. Acknowledge the concern first: Validate their feelings to build rapport. Say something like "I get it, showing empathy can feel exposing, especially when past experiences have made it seem like it opens the door to being taken advantage of."

2. Redefine empathy's role: Gently correct the misconception. Explain: "The truth is, people don't push boundaries because we're kind—they do it when expectations aren't reinforced consistently. Empathy isn't lowering standards—it's connecting on a human level while upholding them. It makes tough conversations more effective, not less."

3. Set explicit expectations: Make accountabilities nonnegotiable and tie them back to shared goals. For instance: "When I check in with empathy, it's because I believe in your potential and want to support your success. That said, our team's deliverables, like hitting that Q4 target, remain the benchmark. If something's blocking you, let's tackle it together, but the timeline holds."

4. Follow through with examples: Reinforce this in action. If a boundary is crossed, respond kindly but firmly: "I appreciate your candor in sharing that challenge, and I'm here to brainstorm solutions. At the same time, we need this report by Friday to keep the project on track. How can we make that happen?"

By modeling this balance, you demonstrate that empathetic leaders aren't soft, they're strategic, resilient, and unapologetically effective. Over time, this approach not only dispels fear, but cultivates a culture where kindness amplifies accountability, leading to stronger results and deeper trust. Leaders who master it report fewer instances of exploitation and higher team engagement, proof that clarity turns potential pitfalls into powerful advantages.

Call to Action

Whether you're a born empath who intuitively tunes in to others' feelings and viewpoints or you're driven to cultivate this life-changing ability, one fact stands clear: Empathy unlocks unparalleled potential. Far from a mere wish list, it's a force that propels you as a leader and reshapes lives in your orbit—from colleagues and teams to your wider community. Dive in with these simple steps to build it today.

Practice active listening in your next interaction: The next time you talk to someone (a colleague, friend, or family member), focus entirely on their words and the emotions behind them, noticing tone, pauses, or excitement. Respond by reflecting back what you hear, with something like "It sounds like you're really passionate about that challenge." This tunes in to unspoken feelings and builds trust.

Express genuine care through a quick affirmation: Think of one person in your circle who's facing a hurdle or celebrating a win. Send them a short message or voice note right now, saying something heartfelt, like "I see how hard you're working on this, and I believe in your potential, you've got this!" This demonstrates unstoppable passion for their value, cultivating the bonds of empathetic leadership.

Pause for perspective-taking reflection: Take two minutes to close your eyes and visualize a recent decision or conversation from someone else's viewpoint. What might they have been feeling or needing? Write down one insight. This simple shift helps you see the world through their eyes, igniting the movement of inspiration and positive change.

"The beauty of empathy lies in its proactive nature—it builds bridges, establishing trust and resilience in relationships that sympathy alone might overlook."

NOTES

NOTES

CHAPTER EIGHT: THE 8TH PRINCIPLE

PERSONAL ACCOUNTABILITY

S tepping into leadership is like entering a giant, transparent fishbowl—every move you make, every word you say, and even your silence is on full display. Your team, your peers, and others are constantly watching, interpreting, and reacting. It's not just about what you do—it's about the chain reaction of every decision, gesture, and pause.

Welcome to leadership: a high-visibility, high-impact role that amplifies your wins, exposes your challenges, and requires your full presence. It's a demanding but deeply rewarding path, and navigating its complexity is part of what shapes you as a leader.

And that fishbowl? It's more than just a spotlight—it's the space where trust is either built or broken. Nothing signals credibility more clearly than accountability. When you take ownership of your choices, acknowledge your missteps, and stand tall in both success and failure, you're sending a powerful message: *I'm all in, I'm consistent, and I won't back down when things get tough.*

But let's be clear: Accountability isn't a one-time act—it's a continuous commitment, reinforced daily through your actions, decisions, and presence. When responsibilities are ignored or mishandled, the consequences go far beyond a single moment. Failing to own your part, shifting blame, or letting issues fester not only damages your reputation but also weakens the trust others have placed in you. One mistake can be forgiven. But when avoidance becomes a pattern, credibility begins to erode—quietly at first, then unmistakably. Over time, people stop questioning a single decision and start questioning your reliability as a leader.

Rebuilding from that point isn't easy. Regaining trust is never a quick fix—it's a long game. It demands humility, consistent effort, and a willingness to show—not just say—that you've learned. The only way forward is to prove, through sustained action, that you're committed to doing better and leading with integrity.

The Lesson of Daniel McConaughey

Daniel McConaughey worked in the community center of LRN Network, a nonprofit dedicated to providing educational resources and mentorship to underserved youth. At thirty-two, he was an exceptional program director, recognized for his ability to coordinate volunteers, secure donations, and ensure programs ran smoothly. His talent for resolving logistic issues and inspiring his team during high-pressure events earned him praise from the board. Yet beneath his confident demeanor, McConaughey carried a flaw: He struggled with personal accountability. He excelled at managing initiatives but often deflected blame when challenges arose, framing setbacks as someone else's oversight.

It started subtly. During a major back-to-school drive, a batch of donated school supplies was delayed due to a mix-up in delivery schedules. In the debrief, McConaughey pointed to the volunteer coordinator, Sara Lopez, for not confirming the delivery timeline.

Lopez, who had been juggling multiple tasks, took the criticism, and McConaughey moved on. Later, a mentorship event fell short of attendance goals due to a miscommunication in outreach efforts, which he attributed to the marketing team's oversight. His staff took notice. In the break room, whispers spread: "McConaughey's great at rallying support, but he's quick to point fingers when things go wrong."

The turning point came during a critical fundraising campaign to expand the nonprofit's after-school programs. A glitch in the donation platform caused a delay in processing pledges, risking the loss of key donors. McConaughey was responsible for overseeing the platform's setup and ensuring the campaign launched smoothly. Amid the crisis, the delay left the team scrambling, with thousands of dollars in pledges at risk.

Back at the office, the executive director, Veronica Wilson, a no-nonsense leader known for her fairness, called McConaughey in to discuss the issue. "Explain," she said, her voice sharp.

McConaughey's instinct kicked in. "Ma'am, the tech team didn't flag the platform issue in time. I assumed they had it covered."

Wilson's gaze was unyielding. "Daniel, I don't care who missed what. I want to know what you did to ensure the campaign was ready."

McConaughey faltered. He hadn't verified the platform's functionality or confirmed the setup with the tech team before the launch. He had assumed everything was in place. Stammering, he tried to justify himself, but Wilson cut him off. "Accountability isn't pointing fingers when a campaign falters," she said. "It's owning the outcome, no matter who drops the ball. That's proactive accountability. You're reacting, and it's letting your team down."

Her words struck deeply. McConaughey left her office, reflecting on every instance in which he'd avoided responsibility. He recognized the pattern: reactive accountability, always after the fact, always focused on self-protection. Proactive accountability, as Wilson described, required anticipating problems, taking ownership, and acting before issues escalated. He had been relying on the former, which was undermining his team's trust.

Determined to change, McConaughey started small. He met with the tech team, not to criticize but to understand their challenges. He learned they were overwhelmed during peak campaign periods, making it hard to test every system thoroughly. Instead of escalating the issue, he worked with them to create a prelaunch checklist for critical platforms. When a minor issue arose with a volunteer scheduling tool, he didn't wait for it to escalate. He flagged it to the tech team, suggested a quick fix, and tested the tool himself before the next event.

His team noticed. Lopez, who had felt the sting of McConaughey's earlier blame, watched him take responsibility for a misstep in a workshop schedule that delayed a session. "Sir, you didn't have to own that one," she said.

"It's not owning it," McConaughey replied. "It's ensuring we're set for the next event."

Months later, a massive fundraising gala coincided with a surge in community demand, pushing the nonprofit's resources to their limits. The stakes were high: A single misstep could jeopardize critical funding and damage LRN Network's reputation. McConaughey, now wired for proactive accountability, didn't hesitate. He thoroughly briefed the tech team, double-checked the donation platform's functionality, and kept the outreach team updated on event progress. When a scheduling conflict threatened to derail a key speaker's appearance, he jumped in to coordinate a solution, ensuring the event stayed on track. The gala was a success, and in the boardroom, Wilson gave him a nod. "Well done, Daniel, I knew you had it in you."

The team's trust solidified as they saw McConaughey not as a lone star avoiding blame, but as a leader who embraced the mission and uplifted them. McConaughey never forgot Wilson's lesson. Proactive accountability wasn't just avoiding mistakes—it was building a team that could tackle any crisis. As LRN Network flourished, he remained prepared, knowing he'd earned his place among them.

Think of the eighth principle as your anchor—keeping you grounded in personal accountability, especially when the pressures of leadership threaten to pull you off course.

1. Proactive Versus Reactive Accountability

Channel your inner leader by embracing proactive accountability, taking ownership before issues arise, setting clear expectations, and leading with intention. Avoid falling into reactive habits, where accountability only shows up after mistakes or problems occur. This principle is especially critical in high-pressure environments where decisions carry weight and visibility. Whether you're managing complex projects, leading diverse teams, or driving key results, this guide will equip you with the mindset and tools to lead confidently, stay ahead of challenges, and build lasting trust through consistent follow-through.

Anticipate Challenges

To succeed in a fast-paced, competitive environment, it helps to think ahead and stay ready for what might go wrong before it actually does. The goal is to develop a proactive mindset—spotting potential bumps in the road early, whether it's a tight project deadline that's slipping, a resource you might not have, miscommunication in the team, or a surprise shift in the market. When you can see those things coming and act before they become big problems, you show up as a thoughtful, reliable leader.

One of the easiest ways to build this habit is by working it into your daily routine. Try looking over your tasks, projects, or goals at least a day in advance. This simple step can help you catch small details—like a missed email, a schedule conflict, or a missing file—that could snowball if left unchecked. Making time for this kind of review trains you to think ahead and deal with problems before they mess up your momentum.

Personally, I've stuck to a pretty basic habit throughout my career: I use a whiteboard to keep my top priorities and tasks front and center. Every day, I take a few minutes to review, update, and think through possible scenarios by asking, *What could go wrong, and what can I do about it now?* If I'm running a project, that might mean having a backup plan for late deliverables or someone being out unexpectedly. If I'm working with an internal customer, I try to anticipate their questions or concerns and prep answers ahead of time. It's all about building flexibility into your day so you can adjust quickly when things shift.

Being proactive doesn't just help you avoid chaos—it also builds confidence. Your team, clients, or stakeholders start to trust that you're always thinking a step ahead. It shows that you're reliable, prepared, and ready to lead even when things get unpredictable. Over time, these small habits add up, creating a workflow that's not just smooth, but also built to handle whatever gets thrown your way.

Own the Outcome

Taking ownership is a nonnegotiable part of being a strong leader—no matter who or what caused the problem. Imagine you're running a key project: Your job isn't just to spot what's wrong, but to jump in, fix it, and keep the team moving forward. Whether you're up against a tight deadline, a tech issue, or a miscommunication, your responsibility is to guide your team through it.

The key is to act fast. If things start slipping off track, don't wait—reassign tasks, clear up confusion, or call in help if needed. And when setbacks happen, focus on solutions, not blame. Say a client deliverable is delayed—own it, reach out to them proactively, and adjust the plan to get things back on course.

Remember, you're operating in a fishbowl, so people are always watching how you respond in tough moments. Leading with accountability and a positive, problem-solving mindset sets the tone for your whole team. In the end, every outcome—good or bad—is part of your leadership story. Owning it all is how you keep progress moving and show that you're in it for real.

Build a Collaborative Team

Strong teams are built on trust, support, and working through challenges together, not finger-pointing. When something goes wrong (and it will), your first move shouldn't be to assign blame. Instead, bring your team in and ask, "How can we solve this together?"

This kind of approach shifts the focus from fault to teamwork and opens the door to new ideas. When your team knows you've got their back—celebrating wins, giving honest feedback, and supporting their growth—they're more likely to step up, take initiative, and give their best.

And when tension comes up (which is normal), guide your team to focus on fixing the issue, not criticizing each other. Teams that trust each other recover faster, solve problems better, and get stronger with every challenge. When everyone feels respected and heard, that's when real collaboration happens—and that's how great results are delivered.

Act Before the Crisis

It's much easier to fix a small issue early than to clean up a big mess later. Whether it's a process that's slightly off, a missing resource, or unclear instructions, don't brush it aside. Small problems can grow fast if they're not addressed.

To be a great leader you must keep an eye on what's going on. Check in regularly with your team and projects so you can catch red flags, like missed deadlines, confusion, or signs of burnout, early. Tools like checklists, reminders, or quick team huddles can go a long way toward staying ahead of problems.

When you're proactive, things run smoother, and people trust that you've got things under control. The best kind of crisis is the one that never happens—and every small step you take today can save you, and your team, a whole lot of stress tomorrow.

2. Reactive Accountability Traps to Avoid

The Blame Game

The instinct to dodge responsibility can be almost overwhelming.

When things go awry or you miss a deadline, the pressure to point fingers often kicks in before anyone can even assess the damage. Early McConaughey threw his coworker Lopez under the bus, and was quick to pin the blame. It was a classic move: Deflect, deny, and duck for cover. But while blaming others might feel like a quick escape in the heat of the moment, it's a short-term fix with long-term consequences. It erodes trust, leaving behind a team that's brittle and dysfunctional.

I've witnessed this dynamic play out in countless workplaces, from factories to corporate offices. One careless finger-pointing can fracture team morale for months, creating an atmosphere where everyone's more focused on covering their tracks than collaborating. Suspicion festers, and suddenly every minor error becomes a battleground for self-preservation.

Even worse are the half-hearted confessions that come when someone's caught red-handed. You know the type: a sheepish, "Yeah, okay, it was me," mumbled as if it was enough to sweep the mess under the rug. That's not accountability—it's damage control. It might appear to be doing something, but it's not solving the problem.

Not long ago, we had a supervisor who was driving a forklift at one of our manufacturing plants who accidentally damaged some new and very expensive equipment. It wasn't intentional, of course, but when he was approached about it, he claimed to know nothing—hadn't seen or heard a thing. It immediately reminded me of Sergeant Schultz from the classic TV show Hogan's Heroes: "I know nothing! I see nothing! I hear nothing!" He even attempted to blame someone else for the incident.

Eventually, we were able to confirm that he was, in fact, responsible. When presented with the evidence, he quickly backtracked on his original story and admitted to the incident. Unfortunately, that confession came too late. He lost his job—but in doing so, he learned a hard truth: Honesty is worth more than even the most expensive equipment.

And yes, had he been forthcoming about the incident by reporting it, he would indeed still have a job.

True accountability is owing to your mistakes promptly, with clarity and sincerity. Step up, even when it's uncomfortable, and say, "I messed this up, and I'm sorry." But words alone aren't enough—genuine accountability goes further. You must demonstrate that you've learned from the error, whether that means double-checking settings next time or seeking out training to fill a knowledge gap. Look, nobody expects anyone to be perfect. You just need to value your team enough to be honest, even when the truth stings.

Shifting the mindset from "Who's to blame?" to "How can I make this right?" is transformative. It's a simple question, but it redirects energy from defensiveness to problem-solving. When you model this behavior, owning your mistakes and focusing on solutions, you set a significant example. Over time, your team will follow suit, and what emerges is a culture where trust isn't just a buzzword but the guiding principle. Mistakes still happen—they always will. But in a workplace where accountability is the norm, those mistakes become opportunities to grow stronger together, rather than wedges that drive the team apart. So, the next time something goes wrong, resist the urge to play the blame game. Step up, own it, and show your team what it means to build trust that lasts.

Excuse Overload

We've all found ourselves in those high-pressure moments, cornered by a mistake or a missed deadline, with the temptation to pile on excuses. While justifications might seem like a quick fix, they inevitably burst under scrutiny, leaving you looking unreliable and untrustworthy. Take the example of when Wilson grilled McConaughey in that tense exchange: McConaughey's knee-jerk excuses didn't just fail to deflect the heat—they actively tanked his credibility, turning a manageable misstep into a self-inflicted wound. Instead of dodging responsibility with flimsy rationalizations, the more brilliant move is to own the moment. Fall on your sword, look the other person in the eye, and say, "I messed up," or "Give me a chance to fix it."

Be sure to include an authentic reason behind the mistake—otherwise, your apology may come across as an attempt to deflect responsibility. For example: "Hey everyone, I want to take a moment to sincerely apologize for the error in the client report I submitted last week. The mistake was mine. I rushed through the final review and failed to double-check some key figures. I realize this caused confusion and may have impacted our credibility with the client. I'm taking full responsibility and have already begun putting safeguards in place to ensure this doesn't happen again." That kind of raw honesty doesn't just disarm criticism, it earns respect and builds trust in a way that no cleverly spun story ever could.

People aren't fooled by weak alibis—they see through the cracks and judge you for trying to hide. So, the next time you feel the urge to weave a convenient tale to cover your tracks, resist the impulse. Keep it real, embrace accountability, and demonstrate to your team that you prioritize integrity over temporary comfort. They'll respect your authenticity far more than a shaky, transparent excuse that collapses under the slightest pressure.

Ignoring the Team

In the early days of his career, Daniel McConaughey's focus on self-preservation over collaboration left his crew feeling sidelined and undervalued. This created a growing undercurrent of resentment that simmered just beneath the surface. A disgruntled team doesn't rally when the pressure's on—instead, they're more likely to vent their frustrations in the break room or, worse, disengage entirely. Low morale doesn't just kill the culture—it breeds costly errors, fuels high turnover, and erodes trust, leaving managers scrambling to patch holes in a sinking ship.

So, what's the fix? Be proactive, not reactive. Start by actually listening to your team—don't just nod along while mentally drafting your next email. Regular check-ins, whether formal or casual, signal that you value their input and care about their experience. Address their concerns promptly, even if it's just to acknowledge an issue and outline the next steps.

Make no mistake, investing in morale is a strategic move. Simple acts, like recognizing a job well done or offering flexibility during a rough week, can pay dividends. These efforts compound over time, creating a resilient, cohesive team that's ready to tackle challenges instead of dodging them.

By embracing proactive accountability, you're building a team that's loyal, motivated, and ready to salute your leadership. Ignore them, and you're flirting with a breakdown that no amount of charisma can fix. Choose wisely, and you'll turn a potential liability into your greatest asset.

Overcoming the Barriers

Adopting proactive accountability, where leaders and teams take ownership of outcomes, anticipate issues, and act decisively, can transform organizations, but it's not without hurdles. Many leaders encounter resistance rooted in organizational habits or entrenched cultures. By addressing these proactively, leaders can build resilient teams that thrive on responsibility rather than retreat from it.

Barrier: Fear of consequences

In numerous workplaces, a culture of blame prevails. When mistakes or failures provoke harsh repercussions, such as public shaming, career setbacks, or tarnished reputations, people naturally shift into self-preservation mode. This anxiety results in evasion tactics like concealing issues, postponing choices, or shifting responsibility to dodge fallout. For managers, this dynamic not only hampers daring endeavors but also undermines confidence, perpetuating a loop of concealment and subpar performance.

Strategy: Foster a supportive culture

Shift the focus from strict discipline to real collaboration by building psychological safety at every level of the organization. Start by leading with openness—during team check-ins or meetings, share a personal mistake like: "I misjudged the rollout schedule—here's what I learned from it." Framing it this way shows that taking responsibility isn't a weakness—it's a way for everyone to grow together.

To help people speak up early about problems, set up regular habits like weekly *blame-free huddles* where team members can flag risks without worrying about being blamed. Keep the focus on solving issues, not pointing fingers. You can also introduce *no-fault retrospectives* after projects.

These are structured sessions where the team looks back on what went well and what could've been better, all in a safe, judgment-free space. The goal is to find patterns, improve processes, and support each other—not assign blame. After each project, collect anonymous feedback on what worked and what didn't. Then, come together as a team to brainstorm solutions. This approach builds trust, encourages learning, and helps everyone feel like they're part of the bigger picture.

Barrier: Lack of clarity in roles and expectations

Accountability weakens when roles become unclear, resulting in *diffusion of responsibility*, the workplace version of the bystander effect, where individuals hesitate to act because they expect others to handle it. This issue often arises in expanding organizations, where overlapping responsibilities breed confusion and mutual blame.

Strategy: Define and communicate clear expectations

While a traditional job description certainly serves its purpose in outlining individual roles, it often falls short when it comes to capturing the full scope of collaborative responsibilities within a team.

To bridge this gap, I've developed a practical tool that I call a *separation of duties* document. This comprehensive outline clearly defines who owns each key task and deliverable, ensuring everyone understands their primary accountabilities. Beyond that, it incorporates details on cross-training, specifying which team members are equipped to step in as reliable backups—whether for planned vacations, sudden illnesses, or other unexpected disruptions.

In practice, this approach shines during moments of turmoil, such as when deadlines slip or processes start to unravel, and the inevitable blame game threatens to derail progress. Rather than letting tensions escalate, I pull out the document, facilitate a quick team huddle to review it together, and openly discuss any pain points or evolving needs. If adjustments are warranted, such as reassigning tasks to better align with current workloads or skill sets, we make those revisions collaboratively right then and there. This not only resolves immediate issues but also reinforces a culture of transparency and accountability, turning potential conflicts into opportunities for stronger team alignment.

Call to Action

It's time to step into the spotlight and embrace proactive accountability. No more waiting for feedback or crises to force change. Own your growth, decisions, and impact starting now. Below are a couple of action steps you can take today to help you on your way.

Set one clear goal today: Right now, write down a specific, exciting goal for the next twenty-four hours. Example: Complete the team report draft with innovative ideas by 5 p.m. Break it down into three actionable steps to build momentum and excitement, aligning it with proactive SMART goals that guide you to success.

Take ownership of a current challenge: Identify one immediate obstacle in your work or team dynamic, such as a pending task or communication gap, and address it head-on within the hour. Reach out confidently, propose a solution, and follow through on it. This channels the energy of determination, "plugging the leak" before it floods, to demonstrate commitment and inspire trust.

"Accountability isn't a one-time act—it's a continuous commitment, reinforced daily through your actions, decisions, and presence."

NOTES

NOTES

CHAPTER NINE: THE 9TH PRINCIPLE

EMPOWERMENT

All right, you've made your way through the trials, scaled the peaks of wisdom, and now you stand at the base of the ninth principle of trust: empowerment. This isn't just any principle—it's the capstone of leadership mastery, the one I've kept tucked away for this very moment. Why? Empowering others is the ultimate demonstration of a true leader's trust. Yet, it's also the most overlooked, often left gathering dust due to one problem: a fear of trusting others.

So, let's embark on this grand adventure to unravel the awesomeness of empowerment and cement your legacy as a trust-building legend!

The ninth principle is about releasing control, sharing your knowledge, stepping back, and trusting others to lead. True empowerment means helping people grow their skills so they can accomplish more than they ever dreamed possible. It's that powerful blend of pride and nervousness you feel as you watch them step up and succeed without you. But letting go requires deep trust: trust in their abilities, their judgment, and most of all, their capacity to rise, even if they fail.

This principle is often neglected because extending trust is a tricky proposition. Some leaders cling to control like a life raft, fearing that empowering others might lead to disarray or, worse, make themselves seem less essential. True power lies in lifting others up, not holding them down.

But research shows that giving people more freedom and support actually builds stronger trust. A study involving two thousand employees at a Fortune 500 manufacturing company in the US found a strong link between employee empowerment and trust in leadership. Specifically, employees who felt they had more autonomy, decision-making authority, and access to the resources needed to do their jobs effectively also reported significantly higher levels of interpersonal trust in their managers.[8]

This suggests that when organizations actively empower their people—by giving them responsibility and supporting their growth—they help cultivate a culture of trust where employees feel respected, valued, and confident in their leaders' intentions. When you empower, you're not just building trust—you're forging a legacy. You're creating a team that doesn't just follow but innovates, dares, and thrives. And that, my friend, is the kind of leadership that resonates through the ages.

A Story of Empowerment—Maria's Revolution

Maria Moreno managed the produce section at Country Grocery. For nine years, she demonstrated exceptional skill in organizing, inspecting, and maintaining fresh inventory—her hands precise, her observations keen.

The store was a busy operation, serving hundreds of customers daily and supplying fresh goods to several local restaurants. The work, while steady, prioritized efficiency over innovation. Employees followed set routines, managers focused on maintaining stock levels and cleanliness, and the daily operations moved relentlessly.

Maria distinguished herself on the floor with an unmatched ability to spot spoiled or mislabeled produce, resolving problems quickly and accurately. However, her expertise was often underappreciated by managers and regional supervisors, who saw her as a dependable worker, consulted only when problems became urgent.

One morning, a newly installed automated produce shelving system, meant to rotate stock and reduce waste, malfunctioned. It began bruising delicate fruits and causing stock to pile up incorrectly, leading to delays in restocking and customer complaints. Store managers gathered, debating solutions without progress, while staff waited for direction.

Maria, drawing on her experience with the store's older shelving setups, quickly identified the issue: The system's angle was off, and items weren't sliding properly onto the display trays.

Though previously dismissed by her manager, Ed, Maria understood the cost of delay. She approached the group with calm authority. "The slope of the trays is too steep," she explained. "If we adjust the rack angle, the fruit will settle without bruising."

Ed responded skeptically, but Elliott, a newly hired assistant store manager eager to learn, was intrigued. "What's the exact angle you think it needs?" he asked. Maria gave a precise recommendation based on her experience. Elliott ran a quick check, confirmed her observation, and implemented the adjustment. Within twenty minutes, the issue was resolved and shelves returned to normal operation. Staff expressed their appreciation, and Maria felt a quiet but deep sense of accomplishment.

Elliott approached her. "Your insight was spot-on," he said. "Have you ever thought about moving into store operations or maintenance?" The idea surprised Maria; it felt ambitious. But Elliott's encouragement stayed with her, and that evening, she began researching training programs for grocery operations and facility maintenance.

Not long after, Country Grocery announced a new initiative: an employee-led program to tackle inefficiencies and reduce waste, inspired by recent losses due to equipment downtime. With support from Elliott and others, Maria was invited to join.

At the first meeting, surrounded by managers, technicians, and logistics staff, Maria felt out of place among terms like *inventory optimization* and *cold chain management*. But when the discussion turned to persistent backups in the produce section, Maria spoke up. "The cold case trays in section three are slightly misaligned," she noted. "Quick fixes don't last. A proper alignment and a motion sensor would keep the produce flowing without damage."

There was a moment of silence, followed by a nod from Barbara Delgado, the store director. "Maria, could you map that out for us?" she asked. Though nervous, Maria agreed. Over the next week, she worked with Elliott and others to pilot the solution. The result was that product damage dropped by 60 percent.

Impressed, Barbara approached her personally. "That was outstanding," she said. "We're starting an in-house training program during store hours. Would you be interested?" Maria answered without hesitation: "Absolutely."

Six months later, Maria led a skilled team trained to spot and solve operational problems before they escalated. The store's culture began to shift, collaboration became the norm, and employee voices were genuinely valued.

Maria's insights, once overlooked, became vital to Country Grocery's continued success.

Maria's story illustrates that empowerment isn't just a fancy word—it's a real-life game changer. When you empower your team, you're not just handing out participation trophies—you're igniting a fire that fuels trust, boosts productivity, and builds a culture where everyone feels capable of achieving their goals. Ready to channel your inner empowerment guru? Here's how to make it happen.

Let's dive into crafting the ninth and final principle, accompanied by a guide designed to harness empowerment as a transformative force, enabling you to achieve enduring success.

Authentic Trust

Empowerment starts with trust, and we're not talking the "I trust you to refill the copy machine with paper" kind. Give your team real responsibility—let them own projects, make decisions, and even mess up a little.

Maria's big break came when Elliot trusted her to lead a valued project, and she knocked it out of the park. Show your team you believe in them, and they'll move mountains to prove you right. Begin with a small step. Delegate a task or project you usually control closely or handle yourself, establish clear objectives (like SMART goals), and then step away and wait for the magic to appear.

Tear Down that Wall

To become an empowering leader, don't just cheer from the sidelines—roll up your sleeves and create a space where everyone can excel. Instead of gatekeeping resources or connections, focus on knocking down obstacles and paving the way for your team to grow. Take Maria's story: Her director didn't just say, "You've got this," but went the extra mile, hooking her up with mentors and pulling her into big-deal decisions. That kind of support turns potential into action, helping people build skills, confidence, and networks they might not have otherwise tapped into. You could try something similar, such as starting a mentorship program or inviting your team to attend high-level meetings. A little exposure goes a long way!

For example, I once consulted for a food service company that launched a leadership introduction program where junior employees observed quarterly strategy sessions and even pitched quick ideas or questions. In just two years, participants felt 50 percent more confident in engaging with senior leaders, and 20 percent of them secured more significant roles within the company. That's proof that giving people a peek behind the curtain can make a real difference.

Empowering leadership is a smart move. Teams with genuine opportunities are more energized, creative, and likely to stay. By swinging doors wide open, you not only uplift individuals like Maria, but you also build stronger, more vibrant organizations that everyone wants to be a part of. And let's face it, attracting and retaining talent has become somewhat daunting these days.

Think Outside the Rulebook

Bam! A hefty two-hundred-page employee handbook crashes onto your desk, filled with stiff rules that practically shout, *We don't think you can figure things out!* Nothing kills great ideas like a manual that reads as if it comes from a control freak's diary. Great leaders toss the rulebook aside, allowing the team to dream big, try new things, and maybe even fail. Empowerment isn't a checklist—it's a blank canvas for your team's wildest ideas.

Take Maria, for example. She was an employee in a company that could have easily buried her in protocols. Instead, a senior leader did something radical: They urged her to think outside the box and take risks without fear of a slap on the wrist. No "stick to the script" nonsense. Maria crushed it because she was trusted to innovate and not just follow orders. That's the type of results you can expect from creating a culture where creative risks aren't just tolerated—they're celebrated.

How do you create this? Kick things off with a "No idea's too insane" campaign where your team can unleash their wildest thoughts. Invite them to share ideas. The goal isn't to act on every unconventional pitch but to generate the kind of creative, open energy that promotes brilliant innovations. You'll be surprised how a totally far-fetched suggestion can evolve into something groundbreaking with a bit of room to grow.

Allow me to share a personal anecdote. I collaborated with a team of executives eager to transform our company. We launched the $1,000 Challenge, a simple yet motivating program: Anyone who proposed an idea that met the criteria and was implemented received a $1,000 bonus, with no cap on submissions or recipients.

The response was incredible. Employees who had quietly been sitting on ideas suddenly felt empowered to speak up. One employee suggested a waste reduction campaign that saved multiple resources. Another championed a green packaging solution that lowered expenses and won accolades for eco-friendliness. The best part was that the challenge didn't just generate ideas—it created a culture where people felt valued and trusted to think big.

You don't need a large budget to make this work. Even small deeds, like publicly praising a risky idea that didn't quite pan out, can show your team that originality is a safe bet. The key is to create space for experimentation and to celebrate the process, not just the results. When people know they won't be punished for swinging and missing, they'll swing harder, and that's when the home runs happen.

So, go ahead and loosen the reins. Challenge your team to think beyond the rulebook. Host that brainstorming session, offer a prize for ideas, or simply tell someone like Maria, "I trust you to figure this out your way." You'll be amazed at what happens when you stop managing and start inspiring.

Listen Like a Pro

Empowering leaders don't just command the room with their words—they lean in, listen deeply, and make others feel truly heard. Take Maria, for example. When her ideas were not only listened to but also valued and acted upon, she went from feeling like just an employee to being a trusted partner in the mission. That's the magic of real listening. Creating a culture where every voice, from the wide-eyed newbie's to the seasoned veteran's, carries weight.

When people feel heard, something incredible occurs. They step up, take ownership, and bring their best ideas to the table. It's like flipping a switch from "I'm just here to clock in" to "I'm all in." To make this happen, consider starting *listening tours*. Schedule one-on-one chats or grab a coffee with your team members—keep it casual, not a boardroom interrogation. Ask about their ideas, their career aspirations, life goals, or even their gripes (yes, those matter too). Then follow through. Show them their input isn't just disappearing into a void. A simple tweak based on their feedback can ignite trust and loyalty that endures.

Amplify Positivity as a Leader

Great leaders don't just notice success—they magnify it. They understand that every win, no matter how small, is a chance to reinforce what good looks like and inspire more of it. Where others might give a quick nod or a passing "Nice work," exceptional leaders throw a verbal celebration. They turn recognition into fuel—fuel that powers motivation, boosts morale, and builds a culture of excellence.

Positivity isn't fluff—it's a strategic advantage. When you consistently highlight the right behaviors and outcomes, you're reinforcing the values, habits, and mindsets that drive success. A single genuine shout-out can do more to shape culture than a dozen meetings. It tells your team, *I see you. What you do matters. Keep going.*

Make praise visible and vocal. Use every opportunity to amplify great work:

- Kick off meetings with a quick highlight reel of team wins.
- Create a Wall of Wow in your workspace or digital hub.
- Mention specific names and actions in company-wide updates.
- Send spontaneous texts, voice messages, or handwritten thank-you notes.
- Celebrate milestones—personal and professional—with authentic enthusiasm.

Remember the CARE feedback model (condition, action, result, expectations) from Chapter 5? Years ago, I built a simple tool around it called the Record of Conversation (ROC) form. Originally developed to document coaching and discipline conversations, it quickly became something more powerful—a framework for consistent, positive recognition.

We even took it a step further: We set quotas for positive ROCs. That's right—leaders were expected to formally recognize great performance just as often as they gave constructive feedback. Why? Because positivity shouldn't be random or rare—it should be intentional and expected. When a leader actively looks for what's going right, it shifts their mindset—and their team's.

This helps to create a culture where people feel seen, valued, and motivated to give their best. When positivity is embedded into your leadership style, you're not just managing people— you're mobilizing them. You're creating an environment where confidence grows, risks are embraced, and momentum becomes unstoppable.

Lead with positivity. Make recognition your signature move. Because when you amplify the good, you don't just build a stronger team—you build a team that believes in themselves and feels empowered!

Create a Can-Do Culture

Empowerment flourishes in a workplace that pulses with possibility, openness, and a relentless drive to explore new ideas. Instead of shutting down ideas with the soul-crushing phrase "that's not how we do things," a mantra that smothers innovation and enforces conformity, flip the narrative to "let's figure out how we can make this work." It's the difference between a bolted door and an open window—suddenly, the atmosphere shifts, the room feels brighter, and everyone is eager to climb through to see what's possible. Soon, you'll see a team that transforms from hesitant and reserved into an unstoppable force of innovation, tackling challenges with enthusiasm and ingenuity.

Leading a passionate, engaged team is infinitely more fulfilling than overseeing a group that merely punches the clock, going through the motions with one eye on the exit. When you empower people to bring their whole selves to work—their imagination, their quirks, their gutsy ideas—you're not just building a better team, you're crafting a workplace where ideas take flight, problems morph into exciting puzzles, and every day feels like an opportunity to achieve something extraordinary.

However, this transformation doesn't happen by accident. It takes intentional leadership, consistent modeling, and small daily actions that reinforce an atmosphere of creativity, courage, and collaboration. Here are concrete ways to create and sustain a can-do culture.

From gatekeeper to guide: Too often, managers see their role as protecting the status quo. But great leaders act as guides, not gatekeepers. Instead of saying, "That's not how we do it here," try, "That's a new idea—how could we pilot it on a small scale?"

Encourage experimentation. Even if an idea is 80 percent off base, dig for the 20 percent that might encourage something new. Curiosity is contagious when leaders model it.

Create "what if?" time: Build space for innovation by scheduling regular brainstorming or "what if?" sessions:

- Once a month, hold a no-judgment idea jam where team members can pitch wild, scrappy, or unconventional ideas—no matter how unrealistic they may seem.

- Celebrate the effort to think differently, not just the ideas that get implemented.

This signals that thinking creatively is part of the job, not a hobby.

Reward problem-solving, not just outcomes: Recognize employees who tackle problems creatively—even if the solution doesn't work out perfectly. Set the tone that *We don't punish smart risks. We learn from them.* Use team meetings to highlight stories of courage and resourcefulness, not just final results.

Challenge teams with open-ended opportunities: Instead of giving directives, pose challenges: "Here's the outcome we need. What are some out-of-the-box ways we could get there?"

Invite cross-functional collaboration to promote solutions. This approach fosters ownership, autonomy, and deeper engagement.

Publicly celebrate courageous thinking: Feature *idea spotlights* in newsletters or round table meetings. Shine a light on:

- New ideas that were tested (whether they succeeded or failed).

- Cross-functional partnerships.

- Employees who pushed beyond their job description to innovate.

This become contagious—people see what's celebrated, and they lean into it.

Put it in writing—and action: Where I currently work as the human resources leader, our vision statement includes a powerful commitment: "We believe in being innovative by challenging the status quo."

These aren't just words on a wall, we live them. Leaders across the organization are trained to question assumptions, ask "what if?" before saying no, and model the behaviors that support innovation. One way we hold ourselves accountable is to include innovation behaviors in performance reviews and leadership development plans.

A can-do culture isn't just more fun—it's more effective. It turns hesitant teams into empowered, high-performing teams. It shifts the energy from compliance to creativity. And it lays the foundation for an organization that doesn't just respond to change—it drives it.

Overcoming the Barriers

In my experience as a leader, empowering others has stood out as one of the most challenging yet ultimately rewarding strategies to master. It demands a delicate balance of trust, vulnerability, and foresight, often clashing with our desire for control. Let's explore some primary barriers that hinder effective empowerment and examine strategies to help overcome them.

Barrier: Resistance to change

It is not uncommon for leaders and employees to hold fast to their established routines. Let's be honest: For many, change can feel uncomfortable. Initiatives aimed at empowerment often provoke opposition, as individuals may feel anxious about assuming unfamiliar responsibilities or adhere to the mindset of *we've always done it this way.* The primary cause tends to be inadequate communication. Without a clear articulation of the change's purpose, its broader impact, the value it delivers, and the personal benefits it offers, you can almost guarantee widespread skepticism and outright rejection. I've seen this play out a hundred times.

Strategy: Communicate the why

Don't just tell employees what's going on—get them involved! Invite them to cocreate empowerment programs, turning skeptics into fans. When they're part of the plan, they'll take ownership. Explain the value, not just to the company, but also to the individual. People want to know "What's in it for me?" Test the empowerment proposal in one department first. Watch it unfold, gather those results, and then implement it company-wide.

Barrier: Fear of stumbling

In a workplace where mistakes are met with severe scrutiny, people may hesitate to take risks. This can stifle creativity and prevent ideas from emerging. Worried about failing, individuals may stick to the same old, safe tasks instead of pursuing exciting new paths or tackling interesting challenges. That caution can hinder personal growth and hold the team back.

Strategy: Flop-to-grow

To overcome this challenge, create a workplace that celebrates smart risks and views mistakes as stepping stones to greatness. Inspire your team's courage to try new things by applauding their efforts, not just their successes. And be sure to recognize those who take big swings, even if they don't hit a home run every time.

Barrier: Limited employee engagement

I have often seen people reject the opportunity to take on additional responsibilities, and I am always disappointed, because I am aware that more often than not, this rejection comes from the lack of recognition and appreciation. As a result, employees often experience a sense of disconnection or lack of motivation, which ultimately leads to a diminished interest in embracing new responsibilities or roles.

Strategy: Boost employee engagement with recognition

Pump up the team's energy by honoring every individual's contributions! Cultivate a culture of gratitude through rewards that align with employees' personal values and ambitions. Launch an engaging peer-to-peer recognition program. For instance, encourage each team member to write notes highlighting a positive quality in two colleagues, one from your own department, and one from elsewhere. This activity promotes appreciation, strengthens connections, and deepens your understanding of the people you collaborate with on a daily basis.

As another incentive, offer adaptable work benefits to recognize employees who go above and beyond. "Thanks to Gia's generous overtime last month, our marketing project wrapped up on schedule and exceeded expectations." Gia, we're granting you two flexible floating holidays to use as you wish!

Call to Action

Ready to revolutionize your workplace with visionary greatness, relentless drive, and true empowerment? The fuel for groundbreaking transformation is already inside your team—it's time to ignite it. Here are a few actions you can take today to begin your journey of empowerment.

Identify and empower one hidden talent: Take a hard look at your team today, review recent contributions, observe quieter members during meetings, or engage in informal conversations with frontline staff. Select one overlooked problem-solver, and immediately offer them a small platform, like leading a quick brainstorming session on a pressing issue, to build their confidence and access untapped potential.

Launch a simple feedback platform: To kick-start a culture of open communication, innovation, and empowerment, begin by establishing a straightforward and accessible mechanism for collecting feedback and ideas immediately. This could take the form of a digital suggestion box, such as a dedicated Slack channel or Microsoft Teams thread, where team members can anonymously or openly submit their thoughts, improvements, or creative ideas. Alternatively, opt for a low-tech, high-touch approach such as a quick fifteen-minute end-of-day meeting, either in person or virtual, where everyone shares one quick win, challenge, or idea from the day.

Once the platform is live, make a clear commitment to responsiveness: Review all submissions within forty-eight hours, providing a brief acknowledgment to the submitter: "Thanks for this—it's on our radar!" and outlining any immediate next steps. To build trust and momentum, prioritize action by selecting and implementing at least one viable idea per week. Share updates on progress through a simple weekly roundup in the same channel or meeting, highlighting what was tried, the results, and how it stemmed from someone's input.

Celebrate a small win and delegate autonomy: Recall a recent team achievement, no matter how minor, and publicly acknowledge it with genuine praise, like "Nicely done—you're a rockstar!" Then, assign an entry-level project to a worker-led group, providing clear tools and trust to experiment, thereby promoting ownership and dismantling silos immediately.

Example: Consider launching a project with a self-formed group of three or four volunteers from across departments (marketing, ops, and design, no silos here!). The mission: Experiment with revamping weekly team meetings to make them more engaging and efficient. Ask them to consider innovative formats, such as rotating facilitators, or quick icebreakers, to create fun and productivity.

"True empowerment means helping people grow their skills so they can accomplish more than they ever dreamed possible."

NOTES

NOTES

CHAPTER TEN

RESTORING TRUST

O kay, let's unpack this with a lot of hope and a hint of humor, because restoring trust is like fixing a wobbly IKEA shelf—it's tricky but entirely doable with the right tools and a bit of patience. The 9 Principles of Trust provides a fantastic blueprint for building trust as a leader, but let's not pretend we're all starting with a clean slate. Life can be a bit of a mess. We all have a few relationships in our past where trust has taken a hit, whether it's a colleague you accidentally threw under the bus in a meeting, a friend you ignored during a busy season, or that time you "borrowed" your buddy's car and returned it with a mystery scratch. The elephant in the room? Trust gets dented, and those dents don't just disappear. But I have great news: You can rebuild and restore trust, and it's not as daunting as it sounds.

A Leader's Redemption

It was 2022, and Shelly, a VP at a high-energy tech startup, hit a rough patch with her star team lead, Alex. Their company, a player in the payment platform sector, was growing like wildfire, but things were becoming a bit shaky behind the scenes. Alex, a brilliant yet quiet engineer, was the brains behind a key development team that kept the platform's technology running smoothly. The trouble was that Shelly's leadership missteps had left him feeling sidelined.

It all started when Shelly, racing to hit tight deadlines, brushed off Alex's tech advice. She was all in on speed, pushing a major feature launch despite Alex's warning that it could crash the system. Sure enough, the release flopped, costing the company cash and credibility. Instead of owning up, Shelly pointed fingers at *tech slip-ups* in front of everyone. Ouch. Alex felt hung out to dry, and his team's energy took a nosedive. He clammed up in meetings and stopped tossing out ideas, a far cry from his usual energy.

Shelly noticed the change but figured Alex was just stressed . . . until a top engineer on his team bailed, blaming a trust gap with the higher-ups. That was Shelly's wake-up call—she had to fix things with Alex to keep the team from unraveling.

Shelly took a step back and got honest with herself. She chatted with a mentor, a tech bigwig, who told her to own her mistakes and listen to her team. So Shelly set up a heart-to-heart with Alex—no corporate crap, just real talk. "Alex, I blew it," she said. "I ignored your expertise, and I didn't take accountability when it all went south. I'm sorry." Then she zipped it and let Alex vent about feeling let down. She took it all in without getting defensive.

To show she meant business, Shelly switched things up. She ensured Alex's ideas were at the forefront of tech decisions and even held a team meeting where she acknowledged her role in the outage. It was a bit awkward, but it showed Alex and the crew she had their backs. She also started protecting the team from unrealistic deadlines and gave Alex props for both big and small wins.

Winning Alex back wasn't instant—he was wary at first. But Shelly kept at it, even getting to know him better, like bonding over his love for open-source projects. She greenlit an internal project for him to geek out on, which got him excited and allowed him to shine.

By mid-2023, Alex was back in the game, pitching ideas that improved the platform's reliability. The team was happier, and fewer people were jumping ship. Shelly's efforts to own her mistakes and genuinely connect with Alex turned them into a solid duo, helping the company navigate its next big growth spurt. That whole mess ultimately made Shelly a better leader, with a knack for maintaining a humble and collaborative approach.

A Recipe for Restoration

Shelly's journey provides an insightful example of how quickly trust, that pivotal support (fulcrum) for a relationship, can erode or even snap under pressure. Her story not only highlights how fragile trust can be, but also paints a hopeful picture of the time, patience, and genuine effort required to repair what has been broken. Rebuilding trust isn't a quick fix—it's a slow, intentional process that involves vulnerability, consistency, and a great deal of heart. If you're looking to restore a damaged relationship and revive that sense of connection, here are some practical and thoughtful tips to guide you along the way.

Apologize with Sincerity

When a mix-up or mistake disrupts things, the best way to begin fixing the situation is by owning your part with a genuine apology. Avoid a vague "Sorry" or excuses, and instead be specific about what you're sorry for to show that you genuinely understand. Acknowledge their feelings and share how you plan to make improvements moving forward. For example, instead of a quick "Sorry, my bad," try something like "I'm sorry for spacing out when you were sharing something important. I know that made you feel unheard, and I'll make sure to put my phone down and focus next time." It's a small change that demonstrates you're serious and committed to improving.

Want to dig deeper? Check out Chapter 1, "Open and Honest Communication," for tips on maintaining authenticity and building trust. A heartfelt apology doesn't just smooth things over—it strengthens your relationship. Reflect on what happened, listen to their perspective, and follow through on your promises to demonstrate your genuine apology, paving the way for brighter days together.

To help you convey a sincere apology, self-reflect on your potential blind spots. Ask yourself: *What are my biases? Am I minimizing their feelings because I don't fully understand their experience? Do I tend to prioritize being right over being kind? Have I made assumptions about their intentions without checking in?* These blind spots can quietly undermine your efforts to repair trust, so acknowledging them is the first step toward real emotional accountability.

Listen with Focus

To rebuild trust, create a space where your team's thoughts flow like a river, steady and uninterrupted. Give them the mic and listen with your full attention, avoiding side conversations or quick fixes. Incorporate open-ended questions, like "What's that feeling like for you?" or "How can I show up to support us moving forward?" It's a small gesture that shouts, *I'm here, and I'm all in for your perspective.*

Think of it as active listening turned up to eleven: nodding, making eye contact, and perhaps even a thoughtful "mm-hmm" to keep the positive energy flowing. Feel free to jot down a few notes, but be mindful not to let it distract you from the conversation. To show respect and sincerity, let the other person know why you're taking notes, or better yet, ask if they're comfortable with it.

Keep Showing Up

Trust works like a sturdy bridge you cross every day. When you know it's solid, you step forward with confidence. You build trust when your actions align with your words. Whether you make a small promise or a big one, follow through. If you say you'll send a message, send it. If you promise to be genuine, show up as your true self. That kind of consistency shapes your reputation and tells others, *You can count on me.*

Each time you keep your word, you rack up small wins—like earning loyalty bucks in the currency of relationships. Those wins add up. Over time, they smooth out the rough patches and repair the cracks in your connections. Stay focused on being consistent. It's the everyday effort to be reliable that makes people feel safe and want to stick around.

Want a pro tip? Check out Chapter 2, "Fulfilling Commitments," for a deeper look at why honoring your word supercharges trust. Stick with it, and you'll see your relationships grow stronger—one kept promise at a time.

Be Patient

Think of rebuilding trust like smoking a rack of beef ribs on a lazy Sunday afternoon—it takes time, care, and plenty of patience to get the flavors just right. You can't rush it. Trust needs a slow, steady burn to grow strong again, so don't look for a shortcut to forgiveness or a fast track back to the good ol' days. Those moments will come, but only if you give them room to breathe. Let the other person set their own pace—everyone processes disappointment and recovery differently. Pushing for quick fixes might feel good in the moment, but it's like slapping a Band-Aid on a bullet hole—it won't hold. Instead, focus on the small, consistent steps that show you're in it for the long haul, things like checking in with a kind word, keeping your promises, or just listening without an agenda are the subtle efforts that build a solid foundation over time.

Take a page from Chapter 7, "Empathy," and genuinely try to see things from their perspective.

Celebrate Small Wins

To effectively rebuild trust, think of it as climbing a mountain—it's a steep challenge, but every step upward is a moment to celebrate! So let's keep it light and bring some fun along the way. Celebrate the small wins with a grin. Did you have a conversation that flowed smoothly without a single awkward pause? Bravo! Did you share a laugh over a silly old memory? Awesome! These little moments of connection are like mini celebrations, reminding you both that the relationship still has plenty of joy to offer. But be mindful. These moments are not a one-and-done—they require both persistence and authenticity.

View these small victories as stepping stones, each one bringing you closer to a stronger bond. Chapter 5, "Providing Feedback," reminds us that acknowledging progress with positivity reinforces the good aspects of your relationship. So keep it upbeat, offer a warm nod, and let those small moments of happiness energize your journey together.

Keep Humor Alive

A bit of levity can work wonders. When the moment feels right, slip in a gentle joke, a playful nudge, or a fond memory that always triggers a laugh. Think of that ridiculous private joke that sends you both into hysterics, or how you still reference that one over-the-top movie catchphrase at the worst possible times. Humor is like a ray of sunshine breaking through after a rainy spell—it doesn't erase the clouds, but it reminds you both that joy is still right there, ready to shine. Just be sure to size up the room first—timing is the secret to landing that laugh! For more on this, flip back to Chapter 3, which offers an abundance of tips for keeping humor alive and well!

Call to Action

Trust can be rebuilt with patience, care, and time, even when it is shattered in an instant. Think of trust as our proverbial teeter-totter: A quick jolt might throw it off balance, but it's still in play. Each small effort—a sincere apology, a kind act, a bit of honest conversation, or truly hearing someone—works like a careful step, nudging the teeter-totter back to even. These aren't wild leaps; they are steady, everyday moves rooted in truth that restore equilibrium and often make the bond more resilient.

Here are some actions you can take today to start rebuilding trust.

Offer a sincere apology: Take five minutes to craft and deliver a heartfelt apology via text, call, or in person, taking ownership of your part without excuses. Example: "I'm truly sorry for how my words hurt you. I see that now."

Perform a kind act: Do something small and thoughtful today, like sending a favorite coffee or running an errand, without expecting immediate thanks.

Listen actively and be present: Connect to arrange a relaxed conversation where you give them your undivided attention, eliminate distractions, and paraphrase their feelings: "It seems like that situation left you feeling pretty irritated."

"Think of rebuilding trust like smoking a rack of beef ribs on a lazy Sunday afternoon—it takes time, care, and plenty of patience to get the flavors just right."

NOTES

NOTES

CHAPTER ELEVEN

THE TRUST METRIC

For years, I've relied on the 9 Principles of Trust as my primary framework for coaching and developing leaders. It has served as a dependable roadmap, highlighting the key traits that inspire trust and drive exceptional leadership. However, measuring how well a leader aligns with these principles has proven to be somewhat puzzling. Traditional methods, such as discussing leaders' perceptions of performance or collecting feedback from their teams, often felt cumbersome and inconsistent. Some individuals were very open to providing feedback, while others were more reserved, leaving me with an incomplete picture.

To improve on this exercise, I began experimenting with more structured methods to measure leadership trust. A few years ago, I dipped my toes into anonymous surveys, using tools like SurveyMonkey to create what I called the Leadership Trust

Survey. Each survey was tailored to a specific leader, such as Leadership Trust Survey—Bart Spence. While the questions remained the same each time, using the leader's name allowed me to deliver a dedicated survey and gather feedback focused specifically on that individual's performance.

The surveys utilized statements linked to the 9 Principles, like "This leader communicates openly and honestly." The leader's direct reports would choose from options such as *Always*, *Usually*, *Rarely*, or *Never*, based on their personal experiences. It worked exceptionally well, providing leaders with clear, actionable insights into areas where they were excelling and where they could improve. A recurring pattern emerged: The principle where leaders often scored the lowest was "This leader provides constructive and beneficial feedback." This trend reinforces something I've always said: The absence of solid feedback is one of the primary reasons leaders struggle to inspire and guide their teams.

The early surveys were a goldmine for spotting trust levels, but they had a blind spot: context. Leaders would return with low scores on certain principles, scratching their heads and saying, "Why these marks? What's off?" That feedback motivated me to improve the Leadership Trust Survey.

To crack the *why*, I added a follow-up component to each principal statement. Now, respondents could flag specific areas for improvement, such as whether a leader needed to work on transparency, clarity, or the frequency of their communication. This adjustment was a game changer, helping leaders focus on exact behaviors to refine. As more surveys came in, I noticed an opportunity to explore even deeper by identifying trends across teams, departments, locations, and leadership levels.

That's when the Trust Metric was created, a scoring system designed to quantify trust and simplify comparisons. Each response received a point value: *Always* = 4, *Usually* = 3, *Rarely* = 2, and *Never* = 1. Sum them up, and you arrive at a leader's overall trust score: 9–25 (Low), 26–32 (Medium), or 33–36 (High). This opened the door to various insights, such as identifying if certain principles were consistently weak in specific teams or levels. With this data, organizations could sharply focus their efforts to enhance leadership trust.

Conclusion

As we reach the end of this journey, it becomes clear that leadership is not measured by titles, profits, or performance metrics—it is measured by the hearts we touch, the lives we uplift, and the trust we leave behind.

The 9 Principles explored throughout this book are far more than tools of leadership. They are the language of humanity. They remind us that every workplace, at its core, is a collection of people seeking connection, meaning, and belonging.

Remember, trust is not built in grand gestures, but in the quiet consistency of our actions—the promises kept, the kindness offered, the courage shown when it matters most. It is built every time we choose understanding over judgment, collaboration over control, and vulnerability over perfection.

When you as a leader embrace trust as your foundation, you don't just lead teams—you ignite movements. You create spaces where laughter is heard, ideas are shared freely, and people feel safe to be themselves. Great leaders remind us that work can be joyful, fulfilling, and deeply human.

Business is changing. The world is changing. In a time when uncertainty seems to be the norm, the leaders who will rise are not the ones who cling tightly to control, but those who lead through connection, compassion, and conviction.

Now that you have the tools, I challenge you to make your workplace the most uplifting part of someone's day. Create team meetings that spark creativity instead of anxiety, and lead in a way that ignites a chain reaction of positive change—one that transforms not only your team, but families, communities, and generations to come.

This is what trust makes possible. This is the real work of leadership.

People are hungry for something real, for leaders who see them, who believe in them, and who inspire them to become the best versions of themselves. The 9 Principles of Trust are not a finish line; they are your starting blocks.

As you carry these principles forward, remember this: Every act of trust plants a seed of hope. Every conversation grounded in honesty strengthens the fabric of your culture. And every moment of genuine leadership moves us one step closer to a world where people don't just work for a paycheck—they work to feel a sense of purpose and belonging.

Because when we lead with trust, we don't just build better workplaces.

We build a better world.

ACKNOWLEDGMENTS

Writing this book has been an incredible journey filled with growth, challenges, and countless moments of gratitude. It's been a wild ride, and I'm deeply thankful for the extraordinary people who have shaped my work, perspective, and life. This book reflects their influence as much as it does my own effort. From the bottom of my heart, here's a massive shout-out to those who made this possible.

To God, for blessing me with an extraordinary family, guiding me through every triumph and trial, and giving me the strength to keep going when the path feels uncertain. Your grace has been my compass, and I'm forever grateful for the opportunities and purpose you've placed in my life.

To my wife, Shelby, you are my rock, confidant, and greatest cheerleader. Your endless patience, unwavering support, and willingness to endure my cheesy jokes have been the backbone of this project. You've listened to my half-baked ideas, offered brilliant insights, and kept me grounded when I got lost in the weeds. This book simply wouldn't exist without your love, patience, encouragement, and partnership. You make every day better, and I'm so grateful to be on this adventure with you.

To my three incredible children, Samantha, Sydney, and Mason, you are the heartbeat of my world. Your boundless energy, curiosity, and laughter fill my days with joy, reminding me of what truly matters. Each of you inspires me in your own unique way, whether it's your ideas, your determination, or your ability to make me laugh when I need it most. You're the reason I strive to lead with integrity, build trust, and make a positive impact. Watching you grow into the amazing people you are becoming is my most incredible privilege, and I hope this book makes you proud.

I also want to express my gratitude to the countless leaders, mentors, and teammates, both civilian and military, who have shaped my understanding of trust, leadership, and collaboration. Your wisdom, feedback, and shared experiences have been woven into the pages of this book.

To my readers, thank you for joining me on this journey. Your trust in choosing this book means the world, and I hope it inspires you to lead with courage and foster authentic relationships. Here's to continuing this journey together, building workplaces where trust serves as the foundation, leadership acts as a force for good, and teams achieve their fullest potential.

With all my gratitude,

Bart

SPEAKER

Whether on the page or the stage, Bart Spence helps leaders build workplaces fueled by purpose and trust.

For over two decades, Bart Spence has inspired and empowered audiences worldwide, from Fortune 500 companies to nonprofits and academic institutions. Driven by a heartfelt mission to foster happier, more fulfilling workplaces, Bart brings a unique blend of humor, science, and expertise to every event.

When Bart takes the stage, he fosters an environment of engagement and opportunity. His vibrant, authentic presence blends compelling storytelling with research-backed strategies to captivate and inspire. Audiences don't just listen to Bart's message—they're moved to act with purpose.

When you invest in Bart Spence as a speaker, you invest in your organization's future. His insightful and actionable presentations provide practical tools to elevate workplace culture. Bart's proven approaches have been shown to enhance morale, reduce turnover, and strengthen employee retention, fostering environments where collaboration and innovation thrive.

Partner with Bart to guide your organization toward a brighter, more inclusive, and prosperous future. Let his vision and expertise inspire your team to unlock their full potential.

Contact Bart at Info@bartspencespeaks.com or visit his website: www.bartspencespeaks.com

TRUST SURVEY EXAMPLE

Ready to put the principles of trust into practice?

Scan the QR code below to access a comprehensive Trust Survey designed to help leaders assess the current state of trust within their organization. This survey is aligned with the nine core principles of trust explored in this book and can be used with teams of any size.

Each section includes:
- Targeted questions that surface how trust is experienced across your organization
- Clear alignment to specific trust principles
- Practical insights that highlight opportunities for growth and improvement

Use this survey as a starting point to spark honest conversations, identify blind spots, and begin building a stronger, more transparent, trust-based culture.

ABOUT THE AUTHOR

Bart began his professional journey as a human resources executive, rising through the ranks by mastering the art of unlocking human potential. With over 25 years of experience, he has led transformative initiatives that have reshaped organizational cultures, elevated leadership capabilities, and built high-performing teams. His work spans nimble startups to global enterprises, with over 100 organizations across a wide range of industries, where he delivers data-driven strategies paired with bold, people-centered innovation.

But Bart's influence wasn't meant to stay within the walls of the corporate world. Drawing on his deep HR expertise and natural ability to connect, he has stepped onto the global stage as a public speaker—bringing his insight, passion, and energy to audiences worldwide.

His background in acting, combined with an education in human sciences, adds a unique edge to every engagement, allowing him to command attention and deliver with impact. Whether speaking to a packed auditorium or leading a hands-on workshop, Bart fuses humor, science, and authenticity into every experience. The result? Audiences walk away not just informed, but inspired and ready to act.

Contact Bart at Info@bartspencespeaks.com or visit his website: www.bartspencespeaks.com

ENDNOTES

Chapter One

1   Yufan Sunny Qin and Linjuan Rita Men, "Why Does Listening
     Matter Inside the Organization? The Impact of Internal Listening
     on Employee-Organization Relationships," *Journal of Public
     Relations Research*, 33, no. 5 (2022): 365–86, https://doi.org/10.108
     0/1062726X.2022.2034631.

2   Robin Dunbar, *Grooming, Gossip, and the Evolution of Language*
     (Harvard University Press, 1996).

Chapter Two

3   George T. Doran, "There's a S.M.A.R.T. Way to Write
     Management's Goals and Objectives," Management Review 70, no.
     11 (1981): 35–36, EBSCOhost.

Chapter Three

4   "Stress Relief from Laughter? It's No Joke," Mayo Clinic,
     September 22, 2023, https://www.mayoclinic.org/healthy-lifestyle/
     stress-management/in-depth/stress-relief/art-20044456.

Chapter Four

5   Swati Dir and Tanusree Dutta, "Does Workplace Respect and
     Organisational Identity Matter in Organisations? Exploration and
     Validation Through EFA and CFA," *Psychological Reports* (2025):
     00332941251352396, https://doi.org/10.1177/00332941251352396

.

Chapter Five

6   Andy Kemp, "Organizations Can Redefine Feedback by Including
        Recognition," Gallup Workplace, October 23, 2024, https://www.
        gallup.com/workplace/651812/organizations-redefine-feedback-in-
        cluding-recognition.aspx.

Chapter Seven

7   Ernst & Young LLP, "New EY Consulting Survey Confirms 90%
        of US Workers Believe Empathetic Leadership Leads to Higher
        Job Satisfaction and 79% Agree It Decreases Employee Turnover,"
        PR Newswire, October 14, 2021, https://www.prnewswire.com/
        news-releases/new-ey-consulting-survey-confirms-90-of-us-work-
        ers-believe-empathetic-leadership-leads-to-higher-job-satisfaction-
        and-79-agree-it-decreases-employee-turnover-301397246.html.

Chapter Nine

8   Melinda J. Moyes and Alan B. Henkin, "Exploring Association
        Between Employee Empowerment and Interpersonal Trust in
        Managers," Journal of Management Development 25, no. 2 (2025):
        101–17, https://doi.org/10.1108/02621710610645108.

www.ingramcontent.com/pod-product-compliance
Lightning Source LLC
Chambersburg PA
CBHW060450290526
45791CB00001B/56